A SEX REVOLUTION

Lois Waisbrooker's
A Sex Revolution

With an Introduction
by Pam McAllister

Women in the Lead
Waisbrooker's Way to Peace

new society publishers

ISBN: 0-86571-050-3 paperback.
       0-86571-051-1 hardbound.
Printed in the United States.
Cover Design by Mara Loft

New Society Publishers is a project of New Society
Educational Foundation and a collective of Movement
for a New Society. New Society Educational
Foundation is a non profit, tax-exempt public
foundation. Movement for a New Society is a network
of small groups and individuals working for
fundamental social change through nonviolent action.
To learn more about MNS write: Movement for a New
Society, 4722 Baltimore Avenue, Philadelphia, PA
19143. Opinions expressed in this book do not
necessarily represent agreed-upon positions of either
the New Society Educational Foundation or Movement
for a New Society.

Women in the Lead
Waisbrooker's Way to Peace

by Pam McAllister

I've been asked to write an Introduction to a book written almost one hundred years ago by Lois Waisbrooker, a long-buried, long-forgotten woman. How ironic: I'm the sort of impatient reader who usually either skips over Introductions altogether or plods dutifully along out of some guilty obligation to the researcher.

Researcher—a dry, distant expert, thin and passionless. Right? Oh dear—I'm the "researcher" this time. But no, it's just me (not at all thin or passionless) wondering where to begin to resurrect Lois Waisbrooker, just me learning the ropes at the library, just me tracking down obscure footnotes and references, thrilled when I make some headway and begin to make the pieces fit, just me wondering how I can bring others along on this rare and fascinating peek at Victorian America's radical side.

Let me be bold, experiment, shamelessly coax along impatient readers tempted to skip my Introduction. I'll document for them my personal observations and some of

> *the feelings the research process*
> *brings up along the way. These*
> *passages, interspersed throughout*
> *the text, will serve as stepping*
> *stones from our time to*
> *Waisbrooker's and, I hope will res-*
> *cue me from the unhappy and*
> *distancing image of "researcher."*

A Sex Revolution was first published in 1893—
forty-two years after Sojourner Truth delivered her
"Ain't I a Woman?" speech, about twenty years after Mother Jones started organizing, thirty-seven
years before Gandhi's Salt March, fifty-two years
before the bombing of Hiroshima. In 1893, America,
exhausted by civil war and expansion, was ready to
burst out of the Victorian Era's tight moral corset
and trade it in for "gay '90s" attire. Elizabeth Cady
Stanton and Susan B. Anthony were nearing the
end of their lives, though passage of the 19th
Amendment granting women suffrage was twenty-
seven years away. Charlotte Perkins Gilman had
just published *The Yellow Wallpaper*; Kate Chopin's
The Awakening would soon see print; Ida B. Wells
was in the thick of her battle, writing, organizing
and lecturing against lynching. In 1893 Margaret
Sanger was fourteen years old; Emma Goldman,
twenty-four.

In 1893 Lois Waisbrooker, the author of *A Sex Revolution*, was sixty-seven. Today little more than a
footnote in the works of doctoral candidates,

Waisbrooker was almost doomed to obscurity by her dedication to the odd integration of anarchism, feminism, free love and spiritualism. She was all but dismissed by the mainstream anarchist movement of her day for her insistence on women's superiority and devotion to the cause of women's freedom. At the same time, she was none too popular with the suffrage-minded women's movement for her advocacy of spiritualism and anarchistic free love.

"Free love," during the Victorian era, referred not to unrestrained lustful pursuits, but to the belief that love and sexual relations should be *free* of coercion from church, state or hedonistic urgings. Sexual relations should be the result of spiritual affinity and love. Spiritualism, like "free love," was considered a challenge to the authority of organized religion because of its emphasis on the individual's direct communication with the spirit world and its teaching that "spiritual affinity" superseded the bonds of legal marriage.

Though she never fit neatly into either the anarchist or feminist movements, Waisbrooker clearly had an enthusiastic if not large following. The editor of *New Generation,* an English birth control journal, dubbed her, "the strongest personality among American feminists."[1] Other contemporaries were inspired to use superlatives as well, calling her ". . . the ablest champion of woman's cause in her sexual and economic relations . . . the still undaunted, unflinching and determined pioneer hero-

3

ine and prophetess of the better time coming . . ."[2] and writing, "I believe that future state will reveal that Mrs. W. has done more to elevate the standard of pure morality, has done more to help bind up the broken heart, and to show men and women how to live and bless the world than nine-tenths of the clergy have done in the past forty years."[3]

Radical lawyer Edward W. Chamberlain, in his review of *A Sex Revolution*, called Waisbrooker "the female Abraham Lincoln,"[4] echoing an earlier observation by law-challenging freethinker Ezra Heywood who recalled seeing Waisbrooker for the first time in 1875:

> I . . . met what seemed to be a Roman Sibyl, Scott's Meg Merrilies, enacted by Charlotte Cushman, Margaret Fuller, and Sojourner Truth rolled into one. . . . She rose, went up the aisle, mounted the platform, and the tall, angular, weird, quaint kind of a she Abraham Lincoln was introduced to the audience as "Lois Waisbrooker."[5]

And when Moses Harman was contemplating a woman coeditor for his anarchist paper *Lucifer the Light-Bearer (Lucifer)*, reader W.G. Markland warned against the danger of creeping respectability and advised, "I regard pugnacity as a desideratum and Lois Waisbrooker has it. . . . Don't call a 'respectable woman' to your aid."[6] What higher praise could be offered one whose pride was her stubborn indifference to the approval of "respectable" society.

4

"SEX CONTAINS ALL": KEY TO
WAISBROOKER'S IDEAS

> *I have been depressed for several*
> *days and cannot get motivated to*
> *work on the Waisbrooker material.*
> *I force myself to go to the New*
> *York Public Library on Fifth Ave-*
> *nue and spend half my time out-*
> *side on the steps beside the grand*
> *stone lions who guard this build-*
> *ing. I make little headway at first*
> *in digging up references to this ob-*
> *scure, forgotten woman, Lois*
> *Waisbrooker. The library has a few*
> *of the early (1890s) issues of* Lucifer,
> *a newspaper devoted to "the*
> *Emancipation of Woman from Sex*
> *Slavery" in which her writings*
> *sometimes appeared. These news-*
> *papers are not on microfilm: they*
> *crumble in my hands.*

The complicated web of Waisbrooker's vision de-
fies linear thinking. For her, *women's superiority* had
to do with *sexuality* which had to do with *spiritualism*
which had to do with *anarchism* which had to do
with *free love* which had to do with *women's superiority*, etcetera. Researchers stumble over themselves
when trying to name her primary area of concern,
calling it "sexual-religious mysticism," "militant

feminism and mystical eroticism," "near-mystical feminism," "sex-radicalism."

Underlying all of Waisbrooker's philosophy was an unflinching faith in the moral force of women, with motherhood being the key to women's superiority. Though Waisbrooker took this notion to new heights, it was somewhat common for advocates of women's suffrage in the mid and late nineteenth century to base their arguments on women's superiority. Elizabeth Cady Stanton, demonstrating a Waisbrooker-like line of thought, articulated just such a sentiment in her diary dated 1890: "We are, as a sex, infinitely superior to men and if we were free and developed, healthy in body and mind, as we should be under natural conditions, our motherhood would be our glory. That function gives women such wisdom and power as no male ever can possess."[7]

Like Stanton, Waisbrooker manipulated the patriarchal bias regarding women's reproductive function upon which so many limitations had traditionally been based, by turning it around to argue for widening women's sphere. In a pamphlet entitled *Suffrage for Woman: The Reasons Why,* Waisbrooker answered those who argued against women's suffrage:

> You assert that there is an essential difference between man's work and woman's. I agree with you most fully. You claim this difference as a sufficient reason for excluding her from the ballot box, from

having a voice in those laws by which she is to be governed: I, on the contrary, claim this difference as one of the strongest reasons why she should have the ballot and all its attendant rights. If her work was the same as man's she could easily be represented by him; as it is not, of course she cannot be thus represented . . .

It is not because he is intentionally cruel that man's work has produced such dire results, but, wanting the proper check, it has been carried to extremes, and sin and death are the natural results of unbalanced, of one-sided conditions . . .

The wonder is that man does as well as he does under the circumstances. Still, this does not do away with the fact that we as a nation are motherless; or, rather, that our mother is but a servant; a petted one to be sure, but nonetheless a servant, is forbidden to act, is unrepresented, is not one of the firm; and man, in trying to be father and mother, too, in trying to do the work of both, has done both poorly, but the maternal part the most poorly . . .

We want women's motherly tenderness, not merely as an influence to plead with, but as a power to restrain; to command man's love to gain hold, when it would walk over the weak and defenseless to the accomplishment of its object.[8]

Waisbrooker was fond of quoting Walt Whitman's observation that "sex contains all." She elaborated on this by repeatedly insisting that sex is the central force in human existence and the fountain of all life, all power: It can bring into being either good or evil as used rightly or wrongly. Rightly, it would be a loving act which would integrate all the physical, intellectual and spiritual aspects involved. The problem is, as Waisbrooker saw it, that sex is held in contempt and vilely misused, thus causing all sorts of hellish misery—prostitution, syphilis (rampant in the 1890s), marital rape, crime and war.

> *Imagine! In the middle of Kansas one hundred years ago, Waisbrooker and other "free thinkers" were publishing articles about marital rape. Moses Harman, editor of* Lucifer, *wrote, for example, "I oppose marriage because it legalizes rape . . ." At first I am excited to discover this. I had thought the current feminist movement was responsible for identifying the crime of marital rape. My excitement quickly fades when I consider that so little progress has been made.[9]*

Waisbrooker consistently blamed the Church for distorting the naturally positive, joyful experience of sex. In "The Curse of Christian Morality," she lambasted the "Christian standard" which decrees, "that under no circumstances may a woman hold the sex relation unless she first pledges herself to some man during life."

. . . Well, what is it that thrills when lovers clasp hands or press lips? It is certainly something: and what can it be but the magnetism flowing from their creative life and blending to create more life for each other?

But the Christian standard of virtue recognizes no such attraction as necessary. The wife who must be "subject to the husband as unto the Lord," gets no consideration for her attractions or repulsions. She is not supposed to feel anything of the kind. She is simply a sex slave.[10]

Waisbrooker was not shy about addressing violence against women, whether it occurred on the battlefield or in the bedroom. In one essay she cited a news item about a Russian village in which Cossacks had killed the men and raped the women.

"Remember, please, that sex is creative on all planes, and then tell me what was created when those sex-hungry wolves forced those women's persons till satiated. Terror and unspeakable anguish on one side, rage and contempt for their victims on the other, what could be created but a sex poison, a moral malaria? . . . this Cossack hell of which I have spoken is but one of many. They exist more or less whenever there is war; and more, every marriage bed unsanctioned by love is a miniature hell . . . and yet we wonder that our prisons and asylums are filled to the overflowing and that disease is everywhere."[11]

I must sign my name and address numerous times and show proof of being who I say I am before I am allowed to look at several of these very old books. The guards watch me carefully and I try to be gentle with this brittle paper. Aside from being nervous about the guards, I grieve that this wonderful literature, written by progressive thinkers almost one hundred years ago, is in such fragile condition. I hold precious fragments, find a letter referring to Waisbrooker written by her contemporary, Matilda Joslyn Gage, another letter from Emma Goldman. History is coming alive for me and at the same time is crumbling in my hands. As I leave the library, one of the guards asks me out. I politely decline.

Waisbrooker believed that she had her finger on the pulse of the world's misery: If only people would cease their contempt of sex which, because we think it so, is degrading, and instead would honor its positive creative power, sex would become nothing less than the vehicle for the redemption of the human race. "Sex is the source of *all* life, *all* power, and when only mutual love relations exist, and no deception practised, crime and disease will soon become unknown."[12] And, according to Waisbrooker's scheme, mutual love relations could exist only under the condition of woman's freedom, though that freedom would have ramifications far beyond the bedroom walls.

It is uncomfortable to read Waisbrooker's occasional mention of "perfecting the race," not to mention that *Lucifer the Lightbearer* eventually became *The American Journal of Eugenics*. Like the other reformers of her day, she used "race" to mean the human race and, while she (again like other radicals of that period) was apparently intrigued by phrenology, her notion of eugenics seems well-intentioned. She grieved that her world was one of misery—crowded asylums and jails, hunger and illness. Her answer (to everything—war, oppression, poverty, illness) was always the same—with women free, babies would be "rightfully conceived and gestated," which would in turn serve to perfect the human race.

According to researcher Hal Sears, anarchist eugenics, the philosophy articulated by Waisbrooker, was based on the notion that a child's character could be prenatally influenced, and therefore "enslaved, male-dominated mothers could only perpetuate a race of slavish humans." Sears also reports that Waisbrooker herself became increasingly uncomfortable with both progressive eugenics and the prenatal assumptions of anarchist eugenics and, in the last years of her life, warned against hereditarianism.[13]

THE STRIKE OF A SEX

One thing about Waisbrooker's story A Sex Revolution *remains a mystery to me. Several times her main character, Margaret Mulgrove, mentions that women had been granted total control over their own bodies several years before, following a women's strike. A strike? Total control over their bodies?! I am deeply puzzled. What could this mean? Had I missed something in American history?*

None of the other reference books I'm using refer to this puzzle in mentioning Waisbrooker's novel, nor do the researchers make much of the book Margaret Mulgrove is given to read, The Strike of a Sex, *which they apparently assume to be a fictional book read by a fictional character. Suddenly it occurs to me to wonder if there had ever been a real book titled* The Strike of a Sex. *I look in the card catalogue and there it is: In 1891, two years before Waisbrooker's* A Sex Revolution, *there was indeed a book published*

with that title.[14] I spend the after-
noon in the main room reading it
from cover to cover. It is a delight-
fully entertaining, bizarre little
story. In the story, the women have
all gone on strike demanding noth-
ing less than that they be granted
total control over their own bodies.

This is it!—the missing piece.
Now, at last, it all makes sense.
Waisbrooker wrote her story in re-
sponse to this earlier work. A
strike resulting in a string of re-
forms just wasn't enough for her:
she demanded a revolution.

A bell rings. Three guards con-
verge on me. "Lady, the library is
now closed. Ya gotta leave." One
takes the book from my hands. I
don't care. I float out of the li-
brary; and oh, I wish I could hug
the lions, but they remain high on
their stone pedesals, aloof, looking
straight ahead. I go home and hug
Emily my cat.

In the twelve years following Bellamy's *Looking Backward* in 1888, over 100 utopian novels were published in the U.S. One which it is safe to assume had a prominent place on Waisbrooker's bookshelf was a comical but radical little fantasy, *The Strike of a*

Sex, written by George Noyes Miller, a member of the "utopian" Oneida Community,[15] and cousin of its founder, John Humphrey Noyes. It is this book that Lois Waisbrooker's character, Margaret Mulgrove, reads before drifting off, like Dorothy in *The Wizard of Oz*, to dream of a great adventure. Readers in 1893, already familiar with the title *The Strike of a Sex*, needed no explanation of the story which so affected Margaret Mulgrove, thus Waisbrooker provided none. This, however, leaves late-twentieth century readers at a distinct disadvantage. Therefore, it is worthwhile to review the novel which, in effect, inspired the writing of *A Sex Revolution*, provided the fictional history on which Waisbrooker's story is based and even became part of its plot.

The Strike of a Sex is narrated by one Rodney Carford who, in his travels, stumbles unawares into a strange town. He notices almost immediately that the men of this town seem to be in a state of disarray, their hair disheveled, their collars undone, their clothes totally buttonless. The men, he tells us, "bore strange marks of carelessness, not to say positive disorder in their attire." Not only that, but Rodney soon notices that the houses of this town also seem to be in a state of chaos: "Dust and confusion seemed to reign unmolested, and the curtains were clumsily fastened as if by unskillful hands." Rodney even begins to sense the mood pervading the town, one of unaccountable gloom, desolation and joylessness.

As observant as Rodney is (we must, after all, give him credit for noticing the state of the curtains and the absence of buttons!), he is slow as molasses at seeing the obvious until he mutters to himself that the town reminds him of Hamelin in the wake of the Pied Piper. Aha! "No sooner had these words passed my lips than, like an electric shock, I remembered that I had not only not seen a child but I had not seen a woman since I entered the town." Very good, Rodney.

So, where are the women? he asks. He's told that every female, newborn and old, rich and poor, sick and healthy, with all the children, barricaded themselves into a walled institution on a hill overlooking the town three months ago and haven't come out since. "They say that the chains which have bound them for unnumbered ages, although artfully garlanded with flowers and called by sentimental and endearing names, are older and more galling than those of any bondspeople on the globe. They have decided that the time has come to throw off those chains." They call it "The Great Woman's Strike."

As Rodney is trying to piece together the story, a handsome, though of course disheveled, young fellow appears and is introduced as Justin Lister, who "was engaged to be married when the strike came on, and what did his best girl do but drop her weddin' dress, half finished as if it were a hot pertater, and leave him like a shot." Poor Justin!

Justin, however, is holding together better than most and has the presence of mind to explain the origin of this strike idea. (Predictably, Rodney has thought to ponder the origin of the tactic before asking about the women's demands. One might observe, as is evident too often in the late-twentieth century, that men frequently treat women's freedom as little more than a topic for intellectual conjecture. Alas.) Justin offers the suggestion that the women borrowed their tactic from the strike of the London dockmen, an event which suddenly forced the whole world to realize "that Labour, instead of being the footstool or fawning slave of Capital as it had stupidly been assumed to be, was easily its master . . ." Inspired by this event, the women suddenly understood that they had as great an advantage as the dockmen did. "Why, good Heavens! the very perpetuity of the race was in their hands. About this time also there was much earnest talk in many periodicals which sprang up, about the 'Brotherhood of Man.' Strange as it may appear, the women suddenly took up the notion that if all men were brothers, all women were nonetheless sisters, and as such should minister to each other like sisters, and protect each other from all harm. This great idea of the Sisterhood of Women, joined with woman's discovery of her real power when in combination, led to the Great Woman's Strike which you see now in progress."

The notion of Sisterhood embraced by these Victorian women is no small thing. They have, in fact, gone so far as to abolish the classification of women as courtesans (prostitutes) to recognize them as victims of patriarchy. "She [woman] clearly recognized the fact, and it was like a revelation to her, that the courtesan was but the extreme victim of an intolerably cruel and satanic dispensation; that the courtesan had been but a little more deeply trodden under foot than her more respectable sister. With this new view, woman utterly discarded the idea that the courtesan was a special sinner to be approached with a moral tract and a condescending kind of forgiveness. The courtesan had been unspeakably sinned against, not only by man but by woman as well, and more, perhaps, than any sufferer from cruelty on the globe, deserved the loving pity and succour of her sisters."[16]

Now, at last, it occurs to Rodney to wonder what it is the women want. Is it the right to vote? No, the men answer—that right was granted almost immediately. The men of the town had realized, within three days after the strike began, that life was not worth living without women and so had been most eager to grant the women whatever they wanted. Well then, is it the right to own property? No, that too had been granted. Are the women continuing the strike to demand that they be eligible for all civil offices? a right to all material advantages? equal wages for equal work? No, no, no!—all of these had been granted. Well, stammers Rodney, what is it the women want?

(Just then a newsboy runs into the street shouting the day's headline—"Complete Collapse of the Corset Industry!")

The women's great demand, we eventually learn with Rodney—what the women are calling their "Magna Charta," and the one demand the men will have to decide by ballot—is nothing less than each woman's "right to the perfect ownership of her own person." Good Lord!

The men have set Monday as the day they will vote to decide whether or not to grant this last demand. And Monday seems an eternity away. Rodney has long discussions with Justin and reads the newspaper, *Bitter Cry*, published by the striking women.

On the day before the vote, the women stage a parade through the town, an event designed to let the men see "in a simple panorama exactly what woman has been up to this day." The men, starved for the sight of their mothers, sisters, daughters, girlfriends and wives, line the streets. And the women pass by: The unmarried women who have been scorned and ridiculed and whose days are lived in poverty pass by; and the courtesans, victimized and used. The "army of unhappily married women" make up the rank and file of the strike and these "tender mothers of all mankind" impress upon the men the mountain of anguish and toil they have borne. A small band of women makes up the section of those who are happily married. The invalids pass by. And lastly march the young maidens whose innocence merely serves to heighten the misery of what has come before and what is almost certainly their doom.

Rodney faints.

The fateful Monday dawns. As the men cast their ballots, a woman rises to speak, making a last minute bid for a future with "the new man and woman, neither oppressing nor oppressed. . . ." The vote is called: the men and women rush into each other's arms.

NOTES ON *A SEX REVOLUTION*

And they all lived happily ever after? No, not so according to Waisbrooker, who picked up where *The Strike of a Sex* left off. It's not that easy, she seems to say. One can't create the new world piecemeal, granting a right here, a reform there. The whole fabric must be rewoven. The strike was empowering for the women and paved the way for the next step—a revolution!

Waisbrooker's women, under the guidance of Lovella, the embodied Spirit of Motherhood, have had time to realize that the "Strike" left untouched the male tradition of war-making. When Selferedo, the embodied Spirit of the Love of Power, blows the trumpet assembling the men to war yet again, the women, in a clever reversal of the tactic used in *Strike*, threaten not to withdraw from the men but to join them—this time on the battlefield! The men are horrified and resentful of this new interference since they had already given in to so much during the women's strike and had expected to be left alone to run the world. But Lovella explains, "If we

19

have the right to our own bodies, how dare you ask us to use them as gestating rooms for sons who must be reared as marks for bullets or for cannon balls?''

Waisbrooker's Lovella doesn't mince words. She scorns the men's objections that they are the women's natural protectors and says, ''How well the nations have prospered under your care, and how well you have cared for the mothers under whose throbbing hearts the nations have marched into existence, let history declare. . . . Your assumptions are without foundation; your methods are failures; something else must be tried, for war must cease.''

At first the men are immune to the women's words. They are not about to give up their warrior tradition so easily. And so they assemble for war. In response, and at a nod from Lovella, the women, one by one, take their places beside their husbands, their brothers. In this simple gesture, they throw the men into a state of utter panic.

> **Speaking of panicky men, it seems that not only did Waisbrooker's fictional men have trouble comprehending the women's action, but that researchers have as well, most notably Hal D. Sears. In an otherwise excellent source,** The Sex Radicals: Free Love in High Victorian America, **he erroneously wrote of** A Sex Revolution,

"Refusing to allow man to continue foolish wars that were based on ideas of patriotism and religion, woman herself prepared to take up arms against the male in order to end wars for all time."[17] This wording is certainly a distortion of the story and, I think, a significant one. For indeed, the women do not threaten to take up arms *against* the men, but rather threaten to stand *beside* the men as, literally, comrades in arms. In Lovella's words, ". . . we have decided that if you go to war we will go with you, that we will share danger and death by your sides, that what God hath joined together we will not permit you to put asunder."

Men have a long tradition of overreacting to women's protests, not only missing the point of the actions but finding a threat of violence where none was intended. One modern feminist has lamented, "The kind of protest we have been able to wage has been, at most, on the level of what males consider to be typical Halloween pranks. But when women commit these acts, they are labeled vio-

> *lent."[18] And if we know our history we will know this rings true. In her autobiography, English suffrage leader Emmeline Pankhurst marveled time and again at precisely this phenomenon, describing one action in which thirteen women walked to Parliament to deliver a resolution: ". . . and surrounding us on all sides were regiments of uniformed police, foot and mounted. You might have supposed that instead of thirteen women, one of them lame, walking quietly along, the town was in the hands of an armed mob."[19]*

The action by Waisbrooker's women is a quiet and subtle act of revolution. By standing *beside* the men who are set to do battle, the women challenge the claim that blood is shed primarily on women's behalf or for their honor. They refuse to let their lives be used any longer to justify or sanction the reliance on violence. They threaten to strike against their role as docile accomplices in war-making with the faith that their threat alone would be enough. By merely standing beside the men so set to do battle, they also call into question the patriarchy's artificial dichotomy of gender-linked behaviors—that men are characterized by the ability (even a disposition for) and permission to use physical violence, sometimes disguised in the role of protector, and that women are characterized by passivity, indecision, helplessness, often in need of being protected. The women, in standing *beside* the men on the battlefield, rip the lie out from under the patriarchal scheme of the Victorian era. They call the patriarchy's bluff and it works.

This gesture is not clearly a pacifist one, though the intent of the gesture seems to be. Lovella goes so far as to boast that the women are willing to "kill other children's mothers or be killed ourselves." But the explanation which follows betrays her intent to exploit the horrifying image of mothers killing mothers to illustrate the absurdity of war and to shock men out of their casual acceptance of it. She is confident that this gesture will startle and not be carried into action. It is an all-or-nothing gesture born of anguish. "The love in woman's heart has suffered till its latent power is aroused, so aroused that it demands redemption or extinction; we repudiate eternal torture."

> *I am sitting on a little knoll in the park with my Waisbrooker notes. Today is August 6th, the anniversary of the bombing of Hiroshima. Everywhere I look is beauty—the land gently sloping toward two ponds and a thousand shades of green as far as I can see, deeper greens in the cool woods*

> *behind me. I sit beneath an old*
> *elm tree whose heavy branches dip*
> *toward the earth. City children fill*
> *the park, jumping rope double*
> *dutch, riding bikes, running back*
> *to their families for more picnic*
> *food. And today is August 6th. Is*
> *it possible to make sense of this?*
> *to live with the contradictions?*
> *How can I, a woman born since*
> *the bomb, relate to the work of a*
> *woman born before the thought of*
> *it?*

A Sex Revolution is an intentionally didactic novel peopled with sentimental characters, a format popular with readers in the 1890s. Waisbrooker used this story as a vehicle to espouse her philosophy on everything from class analysis to the temperance movement though, oddly, there is little here that reflects the prominence of free love in her thinking. Some of the story's themes hold relevance for late-twentieth century readers; others reflect interests unique to the Victorian era.

The Church Berated

Clearly Waisbrooker sought to target the organized Christian Church for critical attention in *A Sex Revolution*. The main character, Margaret Mulgrove, risks hellfire in examining church teachings under the guidance of her Aunt Hobart, an "infidel." It is the truth, unadulterated by church teaching, they seek. And suddenly, familiar religious images are transformed, most vividly the image of the crucified Jesus—"Are not the toiling millions the bleeding hands and feet, and . . . is not the war-demon ever thrusting the soldier's spear into the side of this crucified God, this grand humanity that is capable of so much?" Through Aunt Hobart, Waisbrooker challenges the church's otherworldly focus, asking her readers not to be distracted by fear of a fiery hell after death, but attend to the hells that exist right now on earth, and to seek salvation by empowerment rather than wait for rescue by a supreme being. When Margaret asks how present evils are to be overcome, the infidel answers, "By belief in our own power to accomplish, through the God within ourselves, that which the church expects, waits for a God outside of ourselves to do for us." Clearly the church is portrayed here as a hindrance to the redemption of the world, if not a tool of the people's oppression. Oh, blasphemy!

Women Bonding for Peace

There are two aspects of *A Sex Revolution* which will undoubtedly be of interest to late-twentieth century readers—the goal of peace on earth and the notion of women as a gender-class bonding to achieve it. In this story the two aspects are woven tightly into one theme. Waisbrooker understood that men, in their adherence to the dictates of patriarchy, are heavily invested in war and the warrior tradition, and that only the total interruption of that deeply entrenched pattern could create the environment in which peace might be established on earth.

Waisbrooker identified women both as victims of war and as accomplices guilty of helping to perpetuate the routine and mythology of warfare, but in *A Sex Revolution* she also cast women in the role of tired, mourning mothers, rising from the ashes of endless warfare to protect their children—the people of the earth. It is not enough that the women protest or beg to be heard, for they want a cure, once and for all, not merely a change of evils. Thus Waisbrooker's women propose that the affairs of the world be transferred to their hands in a fifty-year experiment. Little matter that women lack knowledge of government, Lovella shrugs, asking rhetorically, "Has man evolved one that is satisfactory?" By breaking the patriarchal pattern with fifty-years of women's rule, the human race would be given a chance to start over, unburdened by the accumulation of unrelenting war. The hope, as articulated by Lovella, lies with the children who would be gestated and born during the period of women's rule and thus not be blinded by patriarchal assumptions. After this fifty year retribution would come the time to shift the balance in favor of a new equality, new men and women, neither oppressing nor oppressed.[20]

In assessing the situation and to be fair, Lovella waves her hand and conjures the vision of the grand achievements wrought by men—architecture, grand cities, machines, bridges, railroads, inventions, symphonies, great paintings. But then she conjures the other side of the picture, scenes of misery and sufferings which have "resulted from the lack of the mother element . . ." Waisbrooker's Lovella reminds us that reform will not satisfy the women's goal, and that peace on earth means far more than the mere absence of war. "Men point with pride to the asylums they furnish for human wrecks, thinking it an evidence of great humanity on their part. They do not realize in the least the shame of there being a need for such asylums. When the conditions for perfect motherhood are secured, there will be no such need; but until woman revolutionizes society, such conditions cannot be had."

> *My father writes me a sweet, teasing note, asking how my work is coming on the Introduction to the story "about keeping men barefoot and pregnant in the kitchen." Dad is supportive and open to most of the ideas I work with. His joke makes me laugh. It reminds me of science fiction writer Joanna Russ's wry remark that she cannot imagine a two-sexed egalitarian society and doesn't think anyone else can either.[21] And it reminds me of*

*something else . . . something
painful . . . the time I approached
a scholar I admired to ask about
his understanding of patriarchy.
He turned to me in oh so unschol-
arly a way and snapped, "How do
you know a matriarchy would be
any better?"*

"But until woman revolutionizes society . . ."
—Waisbrooker, almost one hundred years ago, understood the significance of women bonding as a
gender-class to establish peace on Earth. She knew
that it was not enough to merely protest war or the
tools of war, but that peace would be the by-product
of a profound change in the way people interact
with each other and with the world, a change that
must of necessity involve the dismantling of patriarchy. She understood that a world that could con-
done sexism and racial prejudice would be a world
of war, that a nation that could tolerate poverty and
hunger would be a nation tolerant of weapons, that
the violence of the battlefield is directly linked to the
violence of the bedroom. Waisbrooker's goal was
the restoration of the web of life and not just the
gaining of rights for women or a temporary cease-
fire in this war or the other.

The web of life. In the last half of the 20th century,
feminists working for peace have devised an effec-
tive guerrilla theater tactic to illustrate the intercon-
nectedness of life. At the site of various nuclear

28

power plants and military depots, women bring skeins of yarn, spools of thread, and, by tying the strings to fences, trees, posts, each other, weave colorful webs symbolic of the vulnerable balance of dependencies between all living things. Usually police or guards are as in sent out with scissors to cut the threads, thus unwittingly but brilliantly playing their symbolic parts in the scheme of things. It becomes a sort of pageant—women spinning, weaving, creating beautiful designs, chanting messages of peace and change, and agents of the patriarchy (both women and men) sadly playing out their part of destroying, ripping, cutting the webs. It is the sort of ritual that would have thrilled Lois Waisbrooker.

Waisbrooker, who once urged women to unite into self-supporting cooperatives,[22] would have been thrilled too to witness this age of women's peace camps such as those in Comiso, Sicily; Greenham Commons, England; Seattle and Seneca Falls, U.S.A.; Mount Fuji, Japan, and elsewhere.[23] Surely she would have rejoiced that the feminist peace movement of the late-twentieth century is advancing the world's experiment with nonviolent resistance. She would have been puzzled, however, by the minimal use of statements regarding women's superiority, women's biological role as natural peacemakers or key references to motherhood. One hundred years ago, Waisbrooker and many of her sister suffragists freely used rhetoric touting the significance of motherhood. As late as 1915, Charlotte

Perkins Gilman invented an all-woman utopia (in *Herland*) where Mothers (with a capital "M"), the "Conscious Makers of People," ruled the population with a protective and all-encompassing maternal love.[24]

Waisbrooker's women, even those whose lives have been distorted by misery and want, are superior beings whose strength lies in creative love, and it is their task to rescue the men from destructive passions. At one point Lovella sighs, "Alas . . . how little you men understand love! With woman in the lead, love's true law will be learned, and man will cease to grovel in the dust of passion, unsanctified either by moral purpose or spiritual life. Then the central, the creative love, out of which all other loves spring, will become a refining instead of a consuming fire."

As the unsteady world pushes on toward the year 2000, feminists are still pondering the significance of motherhood and the extent to which gender determines behavior. Now, however, the finger of accountability is more likely to be pointed at the system of patriarchy and the way in which that system has manipulated and distorted the lives of both men and women and wreaked havoc on the universe. Though Waisbrooker did blame men for the sorry state of the world, she also understood that they were in part victims of their own system: Lovella generously acknowledges men as not only oppressors but oppressed people themselves, saying, "And he is not so much to blame for this; he is held to that plane of life by conditions he cannot break. . . . Poor man, he is to be pitied. Poor wife and poorly organized children—double victims, victims of victims, and what is to be done?" Thus Waisbrooker cannot merely reduce anyone (even a man) to being a one-dimensional representative of a social function. To this extent she embraced the "complicated truth" of which Barbara Deming has written, ". . . if the complicated truth is that many of the oppressed are also oppressors, and many of the oppressors are also oppressed—nonviolent confrontation is the only form of confrontation that allows us to respond realistically to such complexity. In this kind of struggle we address ourselves always both to that which we refuse to accept from others and to that which we can respect in them, have in common with them—however much or little that may be."[25] This is precisely the sort of revolution in which Waisbrooker's characters seem to be engaged: first they refuse to stay within their prescribed role of passive observers and then they ask the men to join in their fifty-year experiment.

> *One painful memory from college is of the day I gave a report in a political science class where I was the only female student. Throughout the course I had listened carefully to my professor and fellow students debate in impressive detail the fine points of the*

"strategic triad," "hard targets," first-strike capability, deterrence, deployment, procurement, balance of power, MIRVs, ICBMs, and MX missiles. On the occasion of my humiliating (why? still?) experience, I stood alone beneath florescent lights and faced several rows of young men who crossed their well-muscled arms over their chests and slouched impatiently at what they correctly anticipated would be an interruption in their cerebral celebration of anything and everything military—young men who had grown up making strange whistling and a-a-a-a staccato sounds in imitation of bombs falling and machine guns. And even before I (with my body's soft curves and a childhood filled with dolls) opened my mouth, it was understood that I would speak a different language.

And indeed I did, though in my preparation I had done my best to legitimize (camouflage?) my position with a liberal dose of academese. I argued that empathic imagination, creativity and a commitment to cooperation and dia-

*logue were the survival skills the
planet needed. I countered the ra-
tionale for military strategies with
an impassioned plea (alien, alien,
and oh so subjective!) that we stop
this dead-end foolishness and learn
to get along. The words had
seemed inspired by common sense
when I'd written them, and I realized too late how naive and foolish
they sounded in this political science classroom, this "real" world
where one learned to use facts and
figures and to speak with convinc-
ing boredom of "calculated risks."
The boys' smirks grew to open
guffaws, and I blushed, hearing
how silly and childish my words
sounded to their ears.*

Class Consciousness

Though Waisbrooker's fantasy, *A Sex Revolution*,
touches on several themes unique to her era, such
as references to phrenology (the belief that the
shape of the skull reflects a person's mental or
moral character), spiritualism and the temperance
movement, there is at least one other primary
theme relevant to modern readers: the significance
of class. With Lovella's assistance, Margaret Mulgrove is helped to observe that "Those whose toil

produces the wealth of the world do not get their share," and concludes, "The system itself must be changed; there is no other way." She reflects on the words of the apostle Paul who said, "There but for the grace of God go I," and significantly changes the wording to, "there but for different conditions . . . " And in an argument with Selferedo, Lovella . . . the embodied Spirit of Motherhood, explains patiently, "The system is at fault, my dear sir, because it leaves the fate of the employee in the employer's hands. Any system which allows one class of people to make it impossible for another class to have direct access to the sources of supply is a false one, not only because of the dependence it involves, but because the natural tendency of such a system is to make the dominant class selfish and tyrannical."

If Waisbrooker's characters are sentimental, her rhetoric is not. Her fantasy, as short and simplistic as it is, is also quite remarkable for the range of sophisticated political insights reflected there.

"WHAT I WANT MOST IS THE POWER TO DO, TO DO."

The details of Lois Waisbrooker's early life are sketchy at best. She was born Adeline Eliza Nichols in 1826; why or when she took the name Lois is only one of the unknowns in her life story. Of her background she wrote, "My early advantages were few.

I did not come of a literary stock of ancestry. My parents worked hard for daily bread, had but little education, and less time to use it . . . "[26] Her mother "could not recollect when she had seen a well day," and died at age thirty-six. Like her, Waisbrooker claimed lifelong ill-health and wrote, "I have seen some days once in a while, one, two, and even three at a time, when it was a glory to live . . . But, Alas! They would not tarry, and the most of my nearly seventy years have been years of weariness and pain . . . "[27]

Weariness and pain notwithstanding, . . . Waisbrooker certainly seemed to sustain a life of hard work and high energy. She had little schooling in childhood and earned her way as a domestic servant, of which she wrote, "I have worked in people's kitchens year in and year out when I never knew what it was to be rested."[28]

At last I have found a photo-graph of Lois Waisbrooker. It is in an obscure journal published in Chicago in the early 1900s, To-Morrow: For People Who Think. *Under her picture is the caption "Lois Waisbrooker as she is today." A determined but frail-looking woman glares at the camera. She has little hair, large protruding ears, thin lips set straight on the horizontal, dark, piercing eyes. I love her.*

In the photo
Lois Waisbrooker
looks something like this.

At the age of twenty-six she resolved to pursue her education, against great odds, so that she could stop working in other people's kitchens. By this time she was "the same as a childless widow," illness and poverty having forced her to give up her children to the care of others. It took her two years of economic and physical hardship to complete a six-month course, but during that time Waisbrooker discovered a world of ideas she'd never known existed, and she loved it. Soon she was teaching Black children and small classes in country schools. With the advent of her teaching career began a long love affair with her own sound mind:

> . . . I must sit Sabbath after Sabbath under the ministrations of an ignorant man, or stay at home; and if the latter, should gain the reputation of being irreligious, and thus lose my influence with the people. I was a teacher of children, he of men and women; but while listening to the platitudes that fell from his lips, the conviction would force itself upon me that I was better qualified to teach that people than he was, with the question, "Why should the fact that I am a woman be a reason that I should not?"—and the result of that summer's experience, of that questioning, is before the world.[29]

It was not until after the Civil War that her life became one of public record when she began lecturing on women's rights, free love and spiritualism, billing herself as an "untrammeled Spiritualist speaker." "I was never popular," she wrote. "When I first began to act as an itinerant speaker my work was mostly done in back neighborhoods in school houses among people who could gather my life force but could give me very little in exchange.[30]

In 1869 she began her writing and in three years she published four books and pamphlets: *Suffrage for Women: The Reasons Why; Alice Vale: A Story for the Times; Helen Harlow's Vow: or Self Justice* (the story of a young woman betrayed and deserted who overcomes many prejudices and hardships) and *Mayweed Blossoms*.

In 1875 Waisbrooker wrote a novel, *Nothing Like It: or Steps to the Kingdom*, which concluded with a dream sequence dramatizing women's economic and sexual bondage to men.[31] In 1879 she wrote *From Generation to Regeneration* and *The Plain Guide to Naturalism*, a tract articulating her belief that sexuality would provide the human race with the key to immortality.

For a while Waisbrooker was an active leader in Boston's free love and spiritualist communities, picking up the pieces when the infamous Victoria Woodhull, who once had run for the U.S. Presidency, repudiated both spiritualism and free love and emigrated to Europe where she eventually married a rich and "proper" gentleman.[32] In the 1890s, as Waisbrooker moved from Clinton, Iowa to Antioch, California to Topeka, Kansas, she published a journal dedicated to "Humanitarian Spiritualism" called *Foundation Principles*. As with everything Waisbrooker touched, this journal advanced a wide variety of political themes including the abolition of rent and profit.

In 1891 Waisbrooker temporarily lost her footing in the mainstream anarchist movement when she endorsed a proposal made by Rachel Campbell in *The Prodigal Daughter* that, at age eighteen, every woman should receive a monthly stipend from the public treasury in recognition of her role in evolution and as a way to free her from dependency on a man.[33] Needless to say, this stand inspired debate and severe criticism. There is little evidence that Waisbrooker persisted in this argument; nevertheless, her writings do reflect the foundation for such a scheme. She advocated "a state of society in which all that tends to the welfare of gestating mothers shall be considered of more value than cathedrals, palaces, bank accounts or any other form of wealth calculated to build up individual or corporate power, or to perpetuate a sect or sects,"[34] and wrote elsewhere, "The feminine is the embodying power of the universe, is the builder. Man, in freedom, will realize this, will realize that the builder has the right to be provided with what is needed."[35]

In 1892, the year before she wrote *A Sex Revolution*, Waisbrooker began to be haunted and harrassed by Anthony Comstock and his fellow "vice-suppressors." The Comstock Act, a federal law passed in 1873, prohibited obscenity from the mails. "Obscenity," however, had never been defined, and so it had fallen to the government's own Special Agent, Anthony Comstock, to apply the law as he saw fit. Under his guidance, the Post Office Department had established independent powers of censorship and confiscation with no due process, banning such works as Tolstoy's *Kreutzer Sonata* and hounding progressive freethinkers and reformers including, eventually, birth control advocate and educator Margaret Sanger.

That year Waisbrooker, aged sixty six, was asked to serve as guest editor of the free love journal *Lucifer* while its editor, Moses Harman, himself aged sixty two, was in and out of jail on obscenity charges. Waisbrooker accepted the job and almost immediately, in her effort to dramatize the ridiculous inconsistencies of the Comstock Act, reprinted an excerpt about horse penises from a Department of Agriculture report. In her editorial she pointed out that the government report contained descriptions which, if applied to human organs, would have been immediately censored. She was right: the issue was barred from the mails.

Waisbrooker's pen wouldn't be stopped. In 1893, the same year she published *A Sex Revolution*, Waisbrooker wrote *The Occult Forces of Sex* and *The Fountain of Life: or the Threefold Power of Sex* (Waisbrooker had a penchant for subtitles), a tract clarifying the spiritual, intellectual and physical dimensions of sexuality. The following year she wrote a new book, billed as a labor story, titled *The Wherefore Investigating Company*. Other booklets written by Waisbrooker around this time were *Anything More, My Lord?* and *Perfect Motherhood*.

There are huge gaps in this puzzle of Waisbrooker's life, missing pieces I still cannot find. For example, I've found only one reference to the "failure of her marriage." What sort of failure was it and whatever became of her husband? Why and when did she change her first name to Lois? Where was she born? Why did she call her son a "heartache" and what became of her other children? What did she think of her contemporaries— Susan B. Anthony and Elizabeth Cady Stanton? Did she read Matilda Joslyn Gage's marvelous exposé of the Church—a work which would have reinforced much of her own thinking? Was she a pacifist?

It is frustrating to be so stymied by such basic questions. Our history books are filled with the minute details of the lives of this king or that, but the lives and lifeworks of women and poor or minority men are lost to us or buried in the fine print of footnotes.

In 1894 Comstock's vice-suppression agents caught up with Waisbrooker again, charging her with obscenity in *Foundation Principles*. In a column titled "Noticed at Last," Waisbrooker wrote of her arrest: "I have lived in these United States nearly seventy years and have at last grown large enough to be noticed. I begin to think I really am somebody when I find myself attacked by so great a nation . . . "[36] In another letter she wrote:

> *Indeed! none of us are a tithe of what we might have been had the full tide of creative power entered into that which gave us being . . .*
>
> *Painfully conscious of this—conscious of the poverty of my own makeup, and with an unceasing heartache because of the imperfections of one who drew his life from mine—now, when the remembrance of my own ignorance and its results stimulates me to do my utmost to arouse people to the importance of this question of questions; now, when my head is whitening for the tomb, some poor, obscene-minded man or woman marks my paper and sends it to those* pure *men at Washington . . . and I am arrested—am under bonds—and liable to go to prison.*
>
> *Well! The sun will still shine, and people will still think. Thoughts will in time become deeds, and the prison walls that enclose martyrs for truth will disappear.*[37]

Waisbrooker was not without support. On the contrary, freethinkers everywhere were outraged by yet another attack by the censors. Edward Chamberlain, in an essay titled "In the Midst of Wolves," wrote, "Neither her age, her sex, her purity of soul, her nobility of purpose, nor a long life of worthy work avail to save her from the stroke of the assassins who, as usual in such cases, misrepresent her as a wanton, frivolous, impure woman."[38]

In a letter to the editor in the December 28, 1894 *Lucifer*, another defender wrote:

> *Her honesty, integrity, ability and purity of life and purpose have never been questioned or doubted by those who know her well. And now that in the decline of life—she is nearly seventy years old and a chronic invalid—she should be arrested as a felon while engaged in her philanthropic and ill-paid work, can only be explained on the theory that there is money or religious or political influence at the back of the prosecution.*

The arrest also brought forth a letter to the editor of *Lucifer* from the then-famous Matilda Joslyn Gage, whose detailed exposé of male collaboration against women, *Woman, Church & State*, had been published in 1893:

> *Church power MUST be made to yield. The church, as I told a priest who called upon me this morning, is the great source of immorality, in its teaching that* woman was made for man, *to be obedient to him, and under "the curse of God."*
>
> *Well, what has struck Mrs. Waisbrooker? Had not heard of it. Does the "church" or the "state" expect to gag the universe?*

I intend to live a good while yet to help put the vile tyrant down. Give us free *thought,* free *speech, a* free *pen, a* free *people.*[39]

For two years Waisbrooker's case was dragged through the courts, a process which took its toll on her health and resources, forcing her to cease publication of the paper. The case of United States vs. Waisbrooker ground to an anticlimactic halt on June 30, 1896 when a motion in arrest of judgment was filed which "asserted that the offense charged was not within the jurisdiction of the court and the facts stated did not constitute a public offense."[40]

This was not the last of Waisbrooker's battles with the Comstock law. In 1901 she moved to the anarchist colony at Home, Washington (known also for its nudists and vegetarians) and published a monthly feminist-anarchist journal, *Clothed With the Sun,* a project she had initiated a year earlier in San Francisco. The assassination of President McKinley in September of that year by self-proclaimed anarchist Leon Czolgosz, inspired a zealous backlash and determination throughout the U.S. to stamp out the "anarchist menace." Thus began a period of official harassment of the Home settlement which caught Lois Waisbrooker in its wake. She was charged with obscenity for an article, "The Awful Fate of Fallen Women," and, at a federal court trial in July, 1902, was found guilty by the jury and fined one hundred dollars by a judge who personally disagreed with the verdict.[41]

Reflecting later on the trial and complaining bitterly that a number of her letters to *Lucifer* had mysteriously failed to reach their destination, Waisbrooker wrote:

> *It was because I said in print and sent through the mail the words: "There is no sin in a mutual, loving relation," unsanctioned by legality; of course, I was fined one hundred dollars . . .*
>
> *I have long felt that I must say this, and the time has come to do so. Now, howl, ye slaves of church and state! Surely, there is nothing so cruel, so infernal, as is the idea that we must sacrifice health and even life to the supposed commands of some supposed God and to statutes founded upon such supposed commands.*
>
> *"What fools we mortals be," particularly those who sit on the boiler of evolution, thinking to hold things back by their puny strength. Yes, fined one hundred dollars for telling the truth, and the telling of that truth was multiplied many times because of that arrest and fine.*[42]

Waisbrooker's dedication was not dampened but heartened by the trial, and the following year she issued two more pamphlets. For one, *Women's Source of Power,* Waisbrooker solicited financial aid from her readers to enable her to send this book to ministers and teachers in need of enlightenment," . . . and help us to hasten the downfall of the prison walls of ignorance and prejudice which shut from the people the light of the rising sun of freedom."[43]

45

The other 1903 publication, *My Century Plant*, revealed the root of Church power and outlined "how to free the earth from sex disease." One reviewer warned people not to order this pamphlet if they were uncomfortable with "plain, unvarnished statements," adding, "To the pure it will seem purity itself."[44]

Waisbrooker left the anarchist settlement in 1904 for Denver. Increasingly tormented by weakness and ill-health, she wrote in frustration, "What I want most is the power TO DO, TO DO."[45] She continued to churn out revolutionary essays, with words increasingly urgent and unflinching. In a 1906 essay she wrote, " . . . I demand unqualified freedom for woman *as* woman, and that all the institutions of society be adjusted to such freedom."[46]

On October 3, 1909, Lois Waisbrooker died, eighty-four years old and penniless, at her son's home in Antioch, California. Her last article, boldly titled, "The Curse of Christian Morality," was published posthumously. Her voice was consistent to the last:

> *Yes, I mean it. Woman has a natural, an inherent right to herself, a right which church and state refuse to allow her to exercise; but the time is coming when she will take that right and refuse to be crushed . . .*

O, mothers of the race! your children are perishing. They stretch their hands to you for help, and where should a child go if not to its mother? Wake up! assert your right to yourselves, and live it. Harken! do you not hear the declarations of the Universal Life whispering through Mother Nature's attractions: "You belong to yourselves!"[47]

FOOTNOTES

1. Hal D. Sears, *The Sex Radicals: Free Love in High Victorian America* (Lawrence, Kansas: Regents Press of Kansas, 1977), p. 231.
2. "Letters," *Lucifer, the Light-Bearer,* Chicago, January 5, 1905, p. 230.
3. "Letters," *Lucifer, the Light-Bearer,* Chicago, August 24, 1893.
4. Sears, *Sex Radicals,* p. 243.
5. Ibid., p. 232.
6. Ibid., p. 229.
7. Elaine Partnow, comp. and ed., *The Quotable Woman: 1800-On* (Garden City, N.Y.: Anchor Press, 1978), p. 30.
8. Lois Waisbrooker, *Suffrage for Women: The Reasons Why* (St. Louis: Clayton & Babington Printers, 1868), pp. 22-25.
9. Regarding the notion of marital rape, Harman wrote, "If Webster is correct when he says rape is 'sexual intercourse with a woman against her will,' then 'rape in wedlock' is almost universal . . . " Moses Harman, "A Free Man's Creed," *The American Journal of Eugenics,* vol. II, no. 5, August, 1908, pp. 202-3;

    And in a letter to the editor, *Lucifer* reader Emma Best wrote, "I am being continually told that 'women must be protected' . . . Yes, we want 'protection'—protection from marriage laws and customs . . . Protection from rape, the only sexual crime . . . protected—as a husband's sacred right—by marriage." Emma Best, "Letter," *Lucifer, The Light-Bearer,* Chicago, April 27, 1905, P. 294.

    Most remarkable was the reprint of a letter, also in *Lucifer,* from W. G. Markland about a woman recovering from a postpartum operation whose husband forced her to have sex, tearing the stitches from her healing flesh. Markland asked, "Will you point to a law that will punish this brute? . . . Can a Czar have more absolute power over a subject than a man has over the genitals of his wife?" For the text and a discussion of the Markland letter see Sears, *Sex Radicals,* pp. 74-76.

10. Lois Waisbrooker, "The Curse of Christian Morality," *The American Journal of Eugenics.*, vol. III, nos. 7-8, January, February 1910, pp. 25-29. This was Waisbrooker's last article, written at age eighty-four and published several months after her death.

11. Lois Waisbrooker, "Oh, I Wish I Could!" *Lucifer, the Light-Bearer,* Chicago, September 13, 1906, pp. 582-83.

12. "Louis [sic] Waisbrooker," *To-Morrow: For People Who Think,* Chicago, August 1906, p. 64.

13. Sears *Sex Radicals*, pp. 120-21, 244.

14. George Noyes Miller, *The Strike of a Sex* (New York: G. w. Dillingham, 1890.)

15. Oneida was an intentional "utopian community" (1848-79) in New York State which experimented with Biblically based communism and complex marriage.

16. Lois Waisbrooker also held this stance on prostitution and, in an 1872 speech said, "Women prostitute their bodies daily to the abuse of legal brutes, called husbands, and *calling themselves virtuous*, shrink from the very touch of the garments of the more womanly woman who is prostituted illegally . . . Spiritualists know all this to be true, and they know also that broken health, diseased, discordant children, are the legitimate fruits of these legal prostitutions—evils fully as terrible as those that arise from illegal prostitution." This quote is from "The Sexual Question and The Money Power: How Shall This Power Be Made to Serve Instead of Ruling Us?" a lecture delivered at the annual meeting of the Michigan State Association of Spiritualists, Jackson, December 12-14, 1872.

17. Sears, *Sex Radicals*, pp. 242-43.

    Sears may have misunderstood a secondary source, James C. Malin, who, in his chapter on Waisbrooker in *A Concern About Humanity: Notes on Reform, 1872-1912 At the National and Kansas Levels of Thought* (Lawrence, Kansas, 1964), wrote of *A Sex Revolution*, "The women then moved in among their menfolk to fight with them." In turn, other researchers have inherited Sears' misreading, such as Dolores Hayden who, in

The Grand Domestic Revolution: A History of Feminist Designs for American Homes, Neighborhoods and Cities (Cambridge, Mass.: MIT Press, 1981), wrote, "Waisbrooker's novel, *A Sex Revolution*, described a society where women threaten to take up arms against men in order to end all wars."

18. Karen Hagberg, "Why the Women's Movement Cannot Be Nonviolent," *Heresies #6: On Women and Violence* (New York: vol. 2, no. 2, Summer 1978) p. 44.

19. Emmeline Pankhurst, *My Own Story* (London: Virago, 1979) p. 98.

20. For other similar proposals that women be granted the opportunity to manage the affairs of the world, read the works of Francoise d'Eaubonne excerpted in Elaine Marks and Isabelle de Courtiuron eds., *New French Feminisms* (Amherst: University of Mass. Press, 1980), pp. 64-67.

> *Patriarchal man is therefore above all responsible for the demographic madness, just as he is for the destruction of the environment and for the accelerated pollution which accompanies this madness, bequeathing an uninhabitable planet to posterity.*
>
> *"The feminist movement is not international, it is planetary," says Carla Lonzi in* Spit on Hegel.
>
> *Thus a transfer of power is urgently needed, then, as soon as possible, a destruction of power.*
>
> *The transfer must be made from phallocratic man, responsible for this sexist civilization, into the hands of the awakened women.*
>
> —from "Feminism or Death"

See also Barbara Stanford's anthology, *On Being Female* (New York: Pocket Books, 1974), which contains a reprint of a 1971 *Chicago Daily News* item, "Let Women Rule the World, Asks Scientist," by Dr. Peter A. Corning of the University of Colorado.

> *In an age when the masculine virtues are becoming less adaptive for our survival, government by women might actually prove to be superior adaptation in evolutionary terms.*

Finally, Sally Gearhart's essay, "The Future—If There Is One—Is Female," in Pam McAllister, ed., *Reweaving the Web of Life: Feminism and Nonviolence,* (Philadelphia: New Society Publishers, 1982), pp. 266-84, argues that 1) every culture must begin to affirm a female future, 2) species responsibility must be returned to women in every culture, 3) the proportion of men must be reduced to a maintained at approximately ten percent of the human race, not by any loss of lives but by increasing the birth of females with male consent.

21. "Reflections on Science Fiction: An Interview with Joanna Russ," *Quest: A Feminist Quarterly,* vol. II, no. 1, Summer 1975, p. 45.

22. Margaret S. Marsh, *Anarchist Women, 1870-1920* (Philadelphia: Temple University Press, 1981), p. 53.

23. For information on these and other women's peace movement actions see:

Alice Cook and Gwyn Kirk, eds., *Greenham Women Everywhere: Dreams, Ideas and Actions from the Women's Peace Movement* (Boston: South End Press, 1983);

Lynne Jones, ed., *Keeping the Peace: Women's Peace Handbook* (London: Women's Press, 1983);

Feminism and Nonviolence Study Group, *Piecing It Together: Feminism and Nonviolence* (Devon, England: Feminism and Nonviolence Study Group, 1983);

Pam McAllister, ed., *Reweaving the Web of Life: Feminism and Nonviolence* (Philadelphia: New Society Publishers, 1982).

24. Charlotte Perkins Gilman, *Herland,* with an introduction by Ann J. Lane (New York: Pantheon Books, 1979).

25. Barbara Deming, "Remembering Who We Are" *Remembering Who We Are* (Florida: Pagoda Publications, 1981) pp. 187-88.

26. Waisbrooker, *Suffrage for Women,* p. 12.

27. James C. Malin, *A Concern About Humanity: Notes on Reform, 1872-1912 At the National and Kansas Levels of Thought* (Lawrence, Kansas, 1964), p. 117.

28. *To-Morrow*, Oct. 1906
29. Waisbrooker, *Suffrage for Women*, p. 13.
30. Sears, *Sex Radicals*, p. 232.
31. Marsh, *Anarchist Women*, pp. 73-74.
32. Sears, *Sex Radicals*, p. 23.
33. Sears, *Sex Radicals*, p. 239.
34. Malin, *Concern About Humility*, p. 125
35. Waisbrooker, "Women and Economics," *Lucifer, The Light-Bearer* August 5, 1899.
36. Malin, *Concern About Humanity*, p. 122.
37. Waisbrooker quoted by Edward W. Chamberlain, "In the Midst of Wolves," *The Arena*, No. LX November, 1894, p. 837.
38. Ibid., p. 836
39. Matilda Joslyn Gage, "Letter to the Editor," *Lucifer, The Light Bearer* August 24, 1894. Gage, who once ranked in fame and importance with Susan B. Anthony and Elizabeth Cady Stanton, was a brilliant thinker. Born the same year as Waisbrooker, her life's work was published the same year as *A Sex Revolution.* Fortunately this great work has been republished. See Matilda Joslyn Gage, *Woman, Church and State: The Original Exposé of Male Collaboration Against the Female Sex*, introduction by Sally Roesch Wagner, foreword by Mary Daly (Watertown, Mass.: Persephone Press, 1980).
40. Malin, *Concern About Humility*, pp. 130-31.
41. Charles Pierce LeWarne, *Utopias On Puget Sound, 1885-1915*, (Seattle, University of Washington Press, 1975) pp. 183-84.
42. Waisbrooker, "Very Strange," *Lucifer, The Light-Bearer* Chicago, May 25, 1905.
43. Ibid.
44. LeWarne, *Utopias*, p. 189.
45. Ibid.
46. Waisbrooker, "Oh, I Wish I Could!" *Lucifer, The Light-Bearer* no. 1074, Chicago, September 13, 1906.
47. Waisbrooker, "Curse of Christian Morality," pp. 26, 27-28.

A Sex Revolution
by Lois Waisbrooker

PREFACE

DEAR READER:—The history of the past shows us that nations rise, go through a longer or shorter period of prosperity and then decay. The ruling motive in the life of nations, so far, has always been the same, the aggressive or masculine. Self-aggrandizement, *our* nation right or wrong, all to be laid upon the national altar in the name of patriotism, a centralizing of wealth and power in the hands of the few at the expense of the many, and the result has always been what? Go, gather together the human wrecks of any one nation and you have your answer.

Now will not this latest and brightest of nations perish also unless methods are changed, unless the social lever is reversed? Already the seeds of decay are taking root; is there not some law through which we may take a new lease on life, and what is that law, if there be such, if it be not that

"WOMAN, TAKE THE LEAD?"

True, woman is already quite prominent, is becoming more so, but she does not seem as yet to realize that with man's methods she will succeed no better than man has done. She must formulate her own methods before her true work can appear. Woman must be free, must refuse to be led, must believe in herself before the evils attendant upon imperfect motherhood can be eliminated, and as I see things, the only hope of our nation lies in this direction.

Let us once rise above the necessity of armies, navies, prisons, almshouses, asylums, etc., then the future will stretch out before us with ever increasing brightness. The first step toward this desirable consummation is to believe that it *can* be done; the next that it *will* be done, and lastly to determine to do it *ourselves*.

L. W.

CHAPTER I

First, a little something about myself. I, Margaret Mulgrove, am a childless widow. My husband, Richard Mulgrove, went into the Union Army at the beginning of our last war and never came out alive. My only child, little Bessie, took the scarlet fever in the second year of my widowhood, and, though employing the most skillful physician in the whole country around, I could not save her. To say that I was desolate does not begin to express the feeling I had.

An aunt, my father's only sister who lived in another state, hearing of my bereavement, decided to come and stay with me awhile and wrote me to that effect. Now my father and mother, in their lifetime (I forgot to say that I was an orphan also) had been good orthodox Christians, and had brought me up to walk in the same path; so when Aunt Hobart wrote me she was coming, I was a little troubled, for I had been told that she was an Infidel.

I believed infidelity to be something awful, and as our community was a very respectable one, to have a woman of that character come among us as my relative, was an affliction I had not counted on, but it could not be helped; Aunt would be there the next day and I must make the best of it. So the next morning I went to work to put things in the best order possible to receive my expected relative.

She came about ten o'clock, a pleasant-faced, white-haired lady toward whom my heart instinctively went out, and in spite of my prejudices I felt that I should love her. She stayed with me several months during which time nothing was said or done which brought up the subject of beliefs. True, I had purposely avoided everything that could lead in that direction, but she did not seem at all inclined to be aggressive.

The Sunday, and in fact the day before she left, our minister's sermon called out some remarks from her that surprised me very much.

"Why Aunt," I exclaimed, "I thought you were an Infidel!"

"And so I am to church theology."

"And yet you have just affirmed your belief in the underlying principle of all church theology."

"How is that?" she asked.

"You said you believe in God manifest in the flesh."

"I said I believed God manifest in the flesh was necessary to the salvation of the race, but I did not say I believed it had already taken place."

"Not taken place! Do you then look for a coming Christ?"

The old lady smiled. "Before you can understand me," she said, "you must learn that a narrow personal application of a general principle is, must be, false. The universal spirit of life can never be manifest in its fullness through, or be embodied in a person, in any one man or woman. When God is manifest in the flesh as I mean, it will be through the race. Man as a race will have become Godlike, will have arisen above his present condition, will be saved, not from future, but from present hells."

"Well, I really cannot understand you, Aunt."

"I mean simply this, my child, when enough of the love, power and wisdom immanent in the deified fountain becomes developed in the race, and in harmonious proportions, then the evils which now afflict humanity will disappear.

"But how is this to be done?" I asked.

"By belief in our own power to accomplish, through the God within ourselves, that which the church expects, waits for a God outside of ourselves to do for us. God, the soul or spirit of the universe, must be manifest in and act through us to the overcoming of all difficulties, to the surmounting of every obstacle that lies in the way of the progress of the race."

"But we are such weak mortals," I said.

"We are weak only through ignorance, weak because we do not know how to handle nature's forces, which are the true God-forces."

Here I involuntarily looked at my hands which were small and delicate, as if to ask: "What can these do toward saving a world?"

Aunt Hobart saw the movement and asked: "How far can you make your voice heard, Margaret?"

"Oh, I have a good strong voice, Aunt."

"But suppose you wanted to call the doctor here immediately, could you stand in the door and call him from his office?"

"You know I could not. Besides, a voice like that, and all possessing it alike, would be a very unpleasant endowment. The noise, the confusion of sounds, with everyone calling at such a distance for whatever they might want, would make a perfect babel."

"What then would you do?"

"I would step across the street to the telephone and call through that."

"So you would make your voice heard after all?"

"Yes, I suppose so." And then I repeated: "Nature's forces are the real God-forces," for I was beginning to get a glimpse of her meaning.

"Yes, the real God-force, a knowledge of one of which will enable you to send your voice hundreds of miles in any direction you choose, provided nature's conditions have been previously complied with; through such knowledge you can extend your personality, your veritable self, in your voice, over a vast range of space, but you are an invisible silence, at every point except where you desire to manifest a Godlike power, but what does that power say?"

"What does it say?" I repeated wonderingly.

"It says, 'Child, obey me, and then command me."

"How? I do not understand."

"Can you speak your message through a telephone unless all the conditions upon which the transmission of the sound depends have been complied with?" she asked in reply.

"Certainly not, Aunt."

"And if everything is right, if the governing law has been obeyed, and you make the effort, can anything prevent your being heard at the desired point?"

"Certainly not," I again said, and then added, "you make things very plain, but it is all so very different from the way I have been taught it bewilders me."

"But you can understand that when you obey the

law, you command the result—command a God-force; is it not so?"

"It seems so," I answered hesitatingly, "but it looks almost like blasphemy to say so; we poor mortals, to talk of commanding God-forces!"

"Nevertheless, my dear child, it is true, and when we, the race, have so come to understand and so learned to obey a sufficient number of those God-forces to cover all human needs, then we shall be able to so command them as to save ourselves from every human ill. Then God will be manifest in the flesh in fact and in deed."

For some little time I sat in silence. I was overwhelmed with the magnitude of the thought. Seeing that I made no reply, Aunt continued:

"You can now understand what Jesus meant when he said that heaven and earth might pass away but not one jot or tittle of the law. The law, not human enactments, but nature's commands, must be obeyed before the desired end can be obtained. The only price current for any and every blessing is perfect obedience to the law involved. No bribery in nature's courts."

"You quote a good deal of Bible for an Infidel," I remarked.

"And why not, Margaret? Because I am an Infidel in the church sense of that term, it does not necessarily follow that I am an Infidel to truth. If you question the fact that nature's laws are immutable, suppose you test the matter in the realm of mathematics. Could you solve even one problem therein if the law involved is not strictly obeyed?"

"No, Aunt, I could not," I hesitatingly replied. "I might work at it as long as I pleased, but I could never obtain a correct result if I violated the simplest rule concerned."

"But suppose you do not violate the simplest rule, what then?"

"Why, the correct result is sure to be obtained; it has to come."

Aunt quietly smiled at my reply, "In other words, you command the result," she said, "and now, my dear, which interpretation honors Jesus the most, the one which the church has adopted, or the one I have given? I refer to his declaration of the necessity of fulfilling the law, of course, though there are many more of his sayings that are just as little understood."

"You are opening up to me a wonderful range of thought," I said in reply, "and I only wish that you had said these things sooner, or that you were going to stay longer."

"Oh, I think I have said enough now to keep you busy with thought for some time to come, and you can visit me after a while and then we can talk more of nature's laws and of such portions of the Bible as shadow them forth."

She left me the next morning, but just before she went she put a book into my hand saying, "Read it carefully, it will give you food for thought." I took the book and laid it aside. I was too full of the train of thought that had been aroused to read then.

While Aunt remained I had gladly devoted every moment to her, but now I was alone, and I could look at what had been said, could examine the sentiments advanced in the quiet of my own room. The first thing I did was to go over what had been said in connection with the telephone. I then took up the telegraph, and I thought if the telephone is an extension of the voice then the telegraph is an extension of the arm.

I next tried to imagine how thousands of bonafide fleshly arms would look extended through the atmosphere in all directions. The picture was too comical; I laughed till the tears came. The next thought was how likely they would be to get tangled, and then another hearty laugh. It was a wonderful school, this method of thinking, but the most important lesson learned was that the invisible is the real, that it is the real self that goes out upon telephonic and telegraphic lines, that the body is but the machine through which the "I am" acts.

Yes, I saw as I had never seen before that the invisible is the real, that spirit, mind, being invisible, could, through a knowledge of nature's invisible forces, control the visible, the tangible. Then the idea of God manifest in the flesh as Aunt Hobart presented it. But what about a crucified God, I asked when I thought of this. If ever I asked questions and received replies, I did then.

The response to the question, "What about a crucified God?" was "Through what feeling has the race suffered the most?"

"Through what feeling?" I repeated.

"Yes, through what feeling; has not that which gives the most happiness when conditions are right, been also the source of the deepest suffering, to-wit love?"

My inner consciousness acknowledged the truth of this and the unknown something continued: "Then has not God, the God of love, been crucified, nailed to the cross of hard conditions ever since the race had an existence?"

This application of the idea seemed so true, so in harmony with that other new idea, new interpretation of the meaning of God manifest in the flesh, that I felt as if a new world had opened up before me, but the reply to my first question continued to roll in upon me:

"Are not the toiling millions the bleeding hands and feet, and are not the thinkers of the ages, those who are in advance of their time, the thorn-crowned temples? Is not the wormwood and the gall ever being pressed to the lips of such thinkers, and further, is not the war-demon ever thrusting the soldier's spear into the side of this crucified God, this grand humanity that is capable of so much?"

I was awed into silence, and then my thoughts turned upon her whom I had always heard spoken of as an Infidel, and I said to myself: "If she is an Infidel where are the Christians?" Again a silence while the words, "A crucified God," "God manifest in the flesh," kept flitting through my brain. Soon again I felt the thought of what, as before said, was my other self or an unseen presence independent of myself. I say felt, for I heard no sound, but the words were as distinct as though I had. Perhaps it would be better to say I saw them.

"There are two things needed to secure the salvation or elevation of the race: power and wisdom. We need the power to do, and the wisdom to know what to do."

"And where is the office of love?" I asked. "I had supposed that to be the redeeming power."

"Love is the creative power; wisdom the true redeemer, and yet they cannot be separated, but we have the love already—love crucified. The allegory, for it is only that, makes Jesus the God of love and then crucifies him. But there was a resurrection, and that resurrection is typical of what must come to the race, a rising out of the grave of ignorance into the light of knowledge, of wisdom. "The resurrected Christ will not appear till in the fullness of time, or till the sufferings, the sad experiences of mankind have evolved the wisdom which will save us from such experiences, and in the meantime the suffering goes on evolving its lessons. This idea is symbolized by the words: 'The sufferings of Christ are fulfilled in his members.' "

"And his members are those of the church," I said.

"Not so. The members of that body are the whole human family, in the heart of every one of which is love enough to save a world if love alone could do it. Who can measure the mother's love for her child. But oh how it has been crucified! But this love of God is slowly rising and will eventually become the wisdom of God, God manifest in the flesh; and then we shall have an evolved, a fully unfolded, redemption."

There was no more, and indeed I do not think I could have borne any more then, but all through that week I kept revolving in my mind what I had heard.

CHAPTER II

The next Sabbath morning I went to church as usual, but somehow, what the minister said seemed tame. I was so little interested I remained at home in the afternoon, and then I remembered the book Aunt had given me. I had not even looked at it. I would get and read it. When I took off the wrapper I read:

"THE STRIKE OF A SEX"

"What a queer title," was my thought, but I opened it and began to read. Page after page was scanned, becoming more and more interesting as I progressed with the reading, and I did not put it down till the last page was finished. I then lay down upon the lounge and tried to think; but soon I became restless and thought I would take a walk, so I arose, threw a veil over my head and passed out the back door through the garden and turned my steps toward the woods.

I walked on for some time without noticing that the country through which I was passing was new, and when I did it did not disturb me in the least, and I still continued to go forward. Presently, as I ascended a little eminence, I found myself overlooking a vast upland plain, upon the border of which I was standing, and near me on the right I saw a man dressed in officer's uniform and holding a trumpet in his hand. As I looked he raised the trumpet to his lips.

"Please don't blow." I heard a voice say, and I noted that the words were an entreaty, the tones a command.

I turned to see from whence the voice proceeded, and near me stood a woman in whom was embodied all I had ever imagined, and more, of womanly beauty, dignity, and power. As I looked upon her I did not wonder that the tones of her voice were commanding, for her very presence was both a benediction and a command; a benediction in that I too was a woman, and a command to make my womanhood a blessing to the world.

"Who are you?" I involuntarily asked.

"I am the embodied spirit of motherhood; men call me Lovella," was her gracious reply.

The man who held the trumpet had paused and was looking at her. "Why may I not blow?" he asked at length.

"Why would you blow?" was her response.

"I would summon the warriors of the nation to defend its honor and prevent its disruption."

"And the cost of all this?" she queried, keeping her eye fixed upon him.

"The cost," he repeated, looking as though that was nothing as long as the object was accomplished.

"Yes, the cost," she persisted, "not to you but to the people; they must pay the bill, you reap the reward."

The man made no reply to this but looked as if he wondered who this woman was who thus presumed to question him.

She continued: "For the sake of a false standard of honor you would imbue the nation in blood. To preserve an unbroken union to rule over, you would make thousands of widows and orphans. A compact of states that must be enforced by the sword had better be broken."

"You are uttering treason; you are an anarchist," he said, again raising the trumpet to his lips.

Lovella stepped nearer and laid her hand on his arm. "If you blow, I must," she said. I then saw attached to her girdle a trumpet of wonderful workmanship upon which was inscribed "The Power of Mother Love." Emboldened by the kindness of her smile, I stepped forward to examine it more closely, when I found it to be composed of myriads of hearts closely cemented by intertwining fibers.

The man paused again and stood looking at the woman.

"Yes, only a woman," she said, in response to his look, "but a woman in earnest. Does it surprise you, sir, that woman who has hitherto worked with man, thought with man, depended upon man, should now begin to work for herself and her children?"

"But why should she work against man to do this?"

"In self-defense and in defense of her children."

"In self-defense! Why man is woman's natural protector."

The look upon Lovella's face when he said this was simply indescribable. I could think of nothing but Whittier's lines:

"With a scorn in her eye that the gazer could feel,
Like the glance of the sunshine when it flashes on steel."

And nothing but the steel of supreme self-assurance could have withstood that look without flinching. Still her reply was as even, as gentle in tone as though speaking to a little child.

"How has man protected us? Where are my sons? Where are my daughters?" she asked.

"Where are they? Is not the land full of them?"

"Not all of my sons are here—five hundred thousand of those who went, at your command, to war with their brothers, have left their bones to whiten southern battlefields, or they have been buried beneath southern soil, and yet you would summon the demon of war to devour still more of them."

The great, strong man quailed before the eye of this woman; still he would not yield.

"Your sons," he said, "you have counted the rebels. Do you, madam, claim as sons those who fell fighting against the flag of our nation and still call yourself a daughter of Freedom?"

"I am not the daughter but the mother of Freedom, and you chain her continually; but what of those who were on the other side, my fair sons of the north?"

"They died nobly, died defending the flag of their country."

"Ah, but they died, were killed, shot down, were starved to death."

Her look forced a reply, "Yes, they died," he repeated hesitatingly.

"Then where was their protection, where the protection of their wives from widowhood, their children from orphanage?"

"It is of no use to argue with a woman," he said, and he lifted his trumpet to his lips and blew long and loud. As he did this Lovella blew also, and strange to say the sound of her trumpet drowned that of his.

The man did not seem to realize this till he had blown a second blast, and then finding that her work neutralized his, he attempted to take her trumpet from her. She only smiled at the futile attempt and waited.

He blew again. She did the same, and at the same moment, but this time she sent out a peculiar note the sound of which had hardly died away when I saw myriads of women coming from every direction. They soon filled one-half the vast plain, while a group of the most advanced among them, judging from their appearance, surrounded the tall 'Spirit of Motherhood.'

"My daughters," she said, "who of you are willing to yield up your sons to fight the sons of other mothers?"

Expressive looks were their only response. Lovella persisted: "Will you not make your wishes known in this matter?"

This time the cry was: "No more war, no more war."

"Wait," said the man. "Do not decide hastily; do not force us to antagonize you; think upon this matter before you decide. What has become of your spirit of patriotism, of that self-sacrifice which has hitherto made women so lovely?" But again the cry was heard, "No more war."

For a little time there was silence, and as I looked upon the vast multitude I remarked to one standing near me, "Another 'Strike of a Sex.' "

"Strike?" she said, looking as though she did not quite understand.

"Yes, the time when you assembled and demanded the right to your own bodies."

"Oh, that is what you call it, a strike; well we find that we must demand yet more in order to make that concession practical. A strike? This is a sex revolution!"

"A sex revolution, what do you mean by that?" I asked. The "Strike of a Sex" had astonished me, but this was yet more, so I awaited her reply with a mixture of curiosity and interest.

"We mean that man's methods must be reversed, that love guided by wisdom shall take the place of brute force."

"You intend then, to take the ruling power into your own hands—our own hands, I suppose I ought to say, as I am a woman too."

She laughed, "You would have to say 'we intend,' to match your amendment, but we intend to show man that there is a better way and to insist that it shall be followed, if you call that taking the ruling power into our own hands. We are determined that our sons shall no longer be sacrificed to man's idea of national honor, national glory. Does killing and killing elevate nations, make them glorious? Does not the wail of bleeding hearts drown the shout of victory as well as the cry of defeat?"

"What you say is all too true," I replied, "but why has not this step been taken before?"

"Because woman has been a slave, and has believed that she must be one; but she is getting a taste of freedom, she is beginning to sense her power."

Here the man again made an effort to impress the assembled multitude of women with the importance of preserving this "glorious nation" intact.

"This nation," he said, "planted by the hand of God in the midst of the waters, and made great through his favor, shall we permit it to be dismembered by a few hot heads with impractical ideas—this nation which God has raised up to reflect his own glory, and to be a light to the nations of the earth—shall we permit it?"

"If God planted this nation," replied Lovella, "he does not need the blood of our sons to nourish it. He is able to take care of it without our help or he possesses no Godlike power, and as for his glory, will it shine the brighter by being reflected through blood? No, we have had enough of war."

"Very well; if this is your final decision, we must act without you. We thought, when we conceded what you asked awhile since, that you would be content, but as we find you are not, we must look after the welfare of that which has been committed to our care in spite of your protests."

"Committed to your care!" And again I thought of Whittier's lines as I saw the look upon Lovella's face. "How well the nations have prospered under your care, and how well you have cared for the mothers under whose throbbing hearts the nations have marched into existence, let history declare." She continued, "Your assumptions are without foundation; your methods are failures; something else must be tried, for war must cease," and the assembled multitude bowed their heads in assent.

"Who is that man?" I asked of the one with whom I had spoken before.

"His name is Selferedo, and he loves power, is in fact the embodied spirit of the love of power, of selfishness," she replied.

"I turned my eyes toward the beautiful woman who stood confronting Selferedo so firmly and yet so quietly, and asked; "Why is she called Lovella?"

"Because she is the embodiment, not of creating, but of protecting love."

"What?" said I. "Is not creating and protecting love one and the same?"

She smiled. "The quickening power which plants the germ," she said, "is masculine, but at conception, protecting love takes it in charge, builds its body from her own, thus making it so a part of herself that from henceforth it is in her care. Look to the history of the past and say if the creative, the masculine principle, protects. But hark, Selferedo speaks again."

I turned and heard him say: "Madam, this is not fair; you have taken a dishonorable advantage of me by drowning the sound of my trumpet with your own. Your followers are here, but you have prevented the calling of mine."

"You have had time enough to call yours since mine came. Why have you not done so, sir?"

"Because I expected you would continue to do as you had already done, madam."

"Try it, sir."

He lifted his trumpet and blew a blast that seemed to me loud enough to raise the dead. Presently I saw coming from all directions multitudes of men; but they seemed surprised when they saw their mothers, wives, sisters and daughters there. "Why are you here?" they asked. "Your places are in our homes." No reply was made to this, but Selferedo said:

"I have summoned you, my sons, to the defense of your country. If you would protect your homes you must repel the invader. All are not needed, so we will cast lots as to who shall go."

They began to prepare for the casting of the lots when Lovella called upon them to listen to her. This Selferedo tried to prevent, but she said, "Sir, you accused me awhile since of unfairness; you have talked to the daughters, why may I not talk to the sons? Have I not the right?" she asked, appealing to those who had gathered at Selferedo's call.

"You have, and we will listen to your words," was the general response, so Selferedo was obliged to submit, though he did so with very bad grace.

"I regret," said she when silence was restored, "that I must correct the statement that has been made to you. It is false; our homes are not in danger; a portion of this confederation of states has decided upon an independent government. This you know was done once before, not by these same states, nor for the same reason, and they were forced back by sword and cannon, but at what a cost. Five hundred thousand of our best men gave their lives; heartbreaking wails of agony went up from hundreds of thousands of homes; widowed wives, orphaned children, maimed men filled the land through all its borders—"

"But our flag was preserved intact," cried several voices.

"Intact, with blood dripping from all its folds! Intact—does that restore the dead to life, does that heal broken hearts?" she replied.

There was no response to this and she continued: "Now as then, our homes are not in danger; now as then we shall be the aggressors; now as then we shall invade other homes if you consent to this war. Let them go in peace. If they can do better alone, we have no right to prevent it, and if they cannot, they will come back of themselves if we leave the way open."

Then, in turn, Selferedo harangued them, brought to bear all the motives, all the influences he could summon. He talked to them of patriotism, of national honor, of their duty to their country, and while he yet held their attention he said: "We will not cast lots but will trust to your patriotism, to your love of country and call for volunteers; all who are willing to resist this attempt to dismember our common country will please step to the front."

There was a moment's hesitation, then one, and another, and yet another took their places, even till there was enough for an army. Selferedo smiled triumphantly. "We have enough," he said.

Lovella turned to the women. "Will the wives, sisters, mothers and daughters of these men come to their sides," she asked.

Immediately there went from among the women to the sides of these men a number fully equal to their own. The men looked up inquiringly. "We have come to go with you," they said in reply.

"No, you cannot go, we do not want women," said Selferedo. "No, no; you must not go," said those fathers, brothers, husbands, and sons.

"We shall go if you do," was the firm but quiet reply.

"But we will not let you go."

"Then you will kill us; for if you go, we shall—or die in the attempt."

I realized then as never before the possibilities of the power of woman's love.

CHAPTER III

"But *we* won't let you go." I saw then as never before the assumption of the position that man takes; taking it for granted as he does that he is woman's rightful ruler. If "and he shall rule over thee" was pronounced upon woman as a curse, the sooner she repudiates such rule the sooner will that curse be lifted. However, there was not much assurance in the faces of the men there present when wives, mothers, sisters and daughters made that declaration. I never saw such an expression. They were speechless with astonishment.

"What does this mean?" said Selferedo, looking at Lovella as if he would like to annihilate her.

"It means, sir, that we are in earnest; it means that we do not intend that the men shall be killed off till large numbers of our women must live alone or violate the law."

"Or violate the law?" he repeated inquiringly.

"Yes; you men make the laws, and you say that a man cannot have but one wife, which is right in itself—is Nature's law where you do not violate her conditions—and then you declare war and the men, many of them, are killed; is that not practically decreeing an equal number of women to celibacy or a violation of natural law and legal statute?"

Selferedo looked as if a new but unacceptable light was dawning on his mind. He evidently felt the force of what she said and could not readily reply to her argument, and she continued:

"In view of all this we have decided that if you go to war we will go with you, that we will share danger and death by your sides, that what God hath joined together we will not permit you to put asunder."

"And leave your children, such of you as have children, motherless?"

"Why not?" she asked. "If you go to war to kill other children's fathers or be killed yourselves, we will go too, and will kill other children's mothers or be killed ourselves."

Selferedo and those with him looked horrified. He opened his lips as if to speak then closed them again; at length he gasped, in the same words he had used before, "What does this all mean?"

"It means that the crucified God is rising from his tomb."

"Not much God in woman's going to war," he retorted.

"You do not understand; men cannot," said Lovella gently. "Woman represents the love element of the God-forces in Nature. Hitherto it has been a negative, a yielding, and consequently a crucified love. The love in woman's heart has suffered till its latent power is aroused, so aroused that it demands redemption or extinction; we repudiate eternal torture."

"Eternal torture," I repeated to myself, "surely woman's life has been little else."

Selferedo did not seem to know what to say to this, but as Lovella made no further remark, he at length asked: "And how much more are you going to demand? As I said awhile ago, when we conceded what you demanded in what you call a 'Strike of a Sex,' we supposed you would leave us alone so far as our way of doing things is concerned."

"I believe you graciously conceded us the right to our own bodies," she said in reply.

"We resigned all rights as husbands and put ourselves in the place of dependents upon your favor."

"What right have you then to demand that we shall bear sons who must go to war, must kill or be killed? If we have the right to our own bodies, how dare you ask us to use them as gestating rooms for sons who must be reared as marks for bullets or for cannon balls?"

"So you intend to separate from us again unless we grant what you demand?"

"Have not these said they will go with you, and die with you, if need be?"

"But that is what we do not want."

"Why not say then in so many words that you want us to rear sons as an offering to the war demon, and daughters whose husbands are likely to be torn to pieces to satisfy that governmental pride which is ready to immolate its citizens on the altar of national ambition? If you persist in declaring war, this is what you mean and why not say it?"

"You are Anarchists, you do not believe in government."

"Wait till you have given us a just government before you accuse us of being opposed to government as such. A just government will be a permanent one, you can rest assured of that."

Again Selferedo was silent, while the vast concourse of both men and women stood waiting the result. At length he said: "But you have not told us how much more you intend to demand."

"How much do you think we ought to demand to make things as they should be?" she smilingly asked. To this there was no reply.

Lovella now turned to the men, who, enthused by Selferedo's eloquence, had volunteered for the war, and asked: "What will you do?"

"What can we do? We cannot see these dear ones die."

"You have enlisted and you cannot go back; desertion is death," thundered Selferedo in his most commanding tones.

"Then we must die, for fight we will not," was the equally positive response.

"And we will die with you," said mothers, wives, sisters and daughters.

"No," said Selferedo, "we do not war on women."

"When you take away fathers, sons, husbands and brothers, you do war on us, and you cannot prevent our dying if they die."

Then there arose a great cry from the men who had not enlisted, and from the women who were with them. They said: "These shall not die for we will not permit it."

Selferedo trembled for he saw that his power was gone, while Lovella said: "War does not tend to the elevation of humanity; on the contrary, it brutalizes, drags us down. Its results are evil, and only evil;

therefore, we demand that war shall cease. Shall our demand be accorded?" and from the vast concourse of men came the response clear and strong: "Your demand shall be accorded." But Selferedo stood silent and rebellious. Lovella read his thought and said:

"You mistake in believing that the glory of our nation has departed because we ignore an insult rather than fight. National duelists are no more honorable than are individual duelists, and the creed of honor once held by them has long since been discarded by gentlemen, by all honorable men. The real glory of our nation has but just commenced; from henceforth the nations of the earth will look to us as taking the lead in beating swords into ploughshares and spears into pruning hooks."

"More Bible," was my thought, and indeed, Lovella seemed to be very familiar with that book, and how much her ideas were like Aunt Hobart's, yet Aunt was called an Infidel. I wish we had more such Infidels. What she and Lovella thought seemed to me to be the highest kind of fidelity to truth, seemed like the butterfly as compared with the worm when put beside past teachings; but, comments aside, I must go on with my story.

Selferedo replied to Lovella's gentle words with: "Time will tell if a nation ruled by women can maintain its position. Judging by her yielding nature, such a nation will become the prey of surrounding nations, will be picked to pieces and divided amongst them: what does woman know of government?"

81

"Judging from the past, you mean; you forget that she is becoming a positive power."

"If she becomes a positive power, in what will her methods differ from man's? How can she maintain her positive position without the sword?"

"You forget, sir, that positiveness and aggressiveness are not one and the same. We pay the nations the compliment of believing them capable of being swayed by moral weapons, if skillfully handled. Besides, as to woman's knowledge of government, has man evolved one that is satisfactory?"

To this Selferedo, as before, made no reply, and she continued:

"Man has had the control of affairs in all of the ages of the past; is it more than fair that there should be a sex revolution?"

"A sex revolution, what do you mean by that?" he asked.

"Let the subservient sex become the dominant one for a time. Man's forte is force; woman's, love. Suppose that force yields the reins to love?"

"Love is a siren; her dalliance leads to death if followed too far," he said contemptuously.

"Alas," she replied, "how little you men understand love! With woman in the lead, love's true law will be learned, and man will cease to grovel in the dust of passion, unsanctified either by moral purpose or spiritual life. Then the central, the creative love, out of which all other loves spring, will become a refining instead of a consuming fire. It will then be like the bush that Moses saw, which burned and was not consumed, a glorifying fire, an uplifting power, a quickener in our search after truth."

The man's reply was a sneer with the words: "Oh, you are very beautiful, but you cannot move me, if you can these others," indicating with his hand the men assembled, "and though defeated now, I bide my time."

"And so can I, to be understood," said Lovella with a sigh, "but I will now try to tell what we demand. I do not like the word, demand, but as you have not heeded our requests, our pleading tears, the force of self assertion must be overcome by the force of love's assertion. We will conquer or die, not for ourselves, but for humanity, so I say we demand. You have conceded to us on the war question, for that it was evil did not need to be proven, and the how to remove it was already plain.

"But there are such other evils that the way to cure them is not yet plain. We demand, not ask, for if they will not do so, we must study them alone—we ask that our brothers study these questions with us, and when the cause of any evil is found, its working clearly understood, we then demand that said cause be removed at no matter what cost, for in the end, its removal will always cost less than its continuance."

"That is, we men must be put in leading strings," said Selferedo, scornfully.

"Why not?" she replied. " 'With what mete ye measure it shall be measured to you again' " is a law of nature. One extreme must bring the other before the balance comes."

For ages past the men have led
  In church, and state, and home,
And battlefields have strown with dead
  To gild ambition's dome,
But now the great transition comes,
  Earth's slaves are being freed,
Love's light is kindling in our homes,
  With woman in the lead.

is the language of one of your own sex, is the
declaration of a sex revolution, and we propose to
make it good, to practicalize it."

"So you propose to run this world for the ages to
come, do you?"

Lovella gave him a look such as a mother might give
to a wayward child: "No Selferedo, only till a balance
is restored, then we can go on together," she said.

"And how long, suppose you, will it take to bring
the balance you talk of?" he asked in the same sneering
tone in which he had so often spoken.

"Live for us as we have lived for you; give us the
aid of your earnest thought, knowing the while that
the decision rests with us, say fifty years, and if the
changes that we bring are not for the better, we will
then concede you your old place."

"Fifty years," he repeated to himself. "Fifty years,
just like a woman's calculation; what can they
accomplish in that length of time?" Then aloud: "Well,
it shall be so; if you think you can do so much in half
a century, you shall have the chance to prove your
power."

"And the credit of what we do will be yours as much as ours, for you have prepared the materials for our work, we shall only arrange it. We could not do what we wish to do but for what you have done."

"If it is creditable," added Selferedo, "we will share the credit with you."

"Would you prefer that it be otherwise than creditable?" asked Lovella, looking him calmly in the face.

"We shall see," he said again, "but remember, it is but fifty years, and at the end of that time I think you will have discovered your folly, if not long before."

There came a sort of mist before my eyes just then, a hazy appearance which I involuntarily tried to brush away. The effort seemed to intensify the difficulty and I wondered what was the matter. Presently, things cleared, but the scene had changed. Instead of a plain filled with women, or even half filled, I was looking into a very large room in which there was a number of both sexes.

Lovella and Selferedo were there, and I seemed to have the power to look into the very soul of the latter. Externally he was as pleasant and agreeable as a man can make himself when he has a purpose to accomplish which he does not wish to have known. To all outward appearances he was as anxious to have Lovella's plans succeed as though they were his own. His manner said: "Fair queen, I am your servant for the next fifty years, and well may you prosper," but the internal thought was, "Yes, your plans shall be carried out and proven so foolish that we men will never have any more trouble from this source. Woman's rights will be a thing of the past, will have been thrown into the waste basket of rejected schemes, and from thenceforth woman will fall back into her proper place, glad to yield the lead to us."

I looked to see if any of the others felt as Selferedo did. Of the some two or three dozen men present there were five who had positions of wealth and honor, were chosen rulers of the people. Of these, four shared Selferedo's feelings, while the other one really hoped that with "woman in the lead," something better would come to humanity. "Four of the five only care for themselves," was my silent comment, when, as if in answer to the thought, I heard the words:

"How hardly shall they who have riches enter into the kingdom of heaven."

I turned to see who had spoken, and if ever there was a divine man in human form, here was one. I looked at him inquiringly, but was too much awed to speak.

"Yes," he repeated, "the kingdom of heaven, the kingdom of love with wisdom as a devoted counterpart. The prophecy of a new heaven and a new earth is no idle dream, but the conditions which will make things new here must be the work of woman, must be born of woman."

Emboldened by his kindly manner, I asked: "Would you accept woman as leader?"

"Most certainly; woman alone can lead man to the divinest heights. Man was first, but the fact that he was incomplete without her showed that he needed a leader. He will finally accord her her true place."

"It would indeed be a grand woman who could lead you," was my thought.

"Yes, grand and more than that is she to whom I owe so much," he said in response, "but listen and learn." Saying this, he vanished.

CHAPTER IV

When I had in a measure recovered from my surprise, I heard Selferedo saying:

"Fifty years will soon be gone; if you would accomplish anything worth the while, you—or I should say *we*, must work fast."

"The best way to facilitate a work is first to understand it," replied Lovella.

"And what do you propose, my fair commander?"

"First of all, a thorough investigation of the machinery of society, both its separate parts, and the effect of one part upon another; and here is where we want the aid of the best, the broadest, the wisest minds of both sexes."

I could see that Selferedo was not well pleased, but he smilingly asked: "And how much of your precious time must we devote to this work of investigation?"

"Enough to master the subject, five, perhaps ten, years."

"But there are some evils, dear lady, the causes of which are so plain there is no need that time be spent to investigate. The fifty years, as I have already said, will soon pass, and I should like to see something done that will tell upon the future. If we can do enough in that time, with 'woman in the lead' to demonstrate her fitness to lead, then there is no more to be said. She will have proved her place. Yet it appears to me like assuming a great deal for her to make the attempt when the best men of the ages have failed to remedy the evils that seem to be inseparable from human nature."

"You forget," she said, "what you men have already done. But for that, we could do no more than the squaw of the wigwam could do if such a work were proposed to her. You have been so intent, however, in evolving wonders from nature's storehouse that you have overlooked their proper adjustment. It takes months to prepare the land, particularly if it be timbered land, and months more for the wheat, corn, potatoes, and whatever else is needed for a good meal, to grow and ripen, but when all is ready, the housewife will prepare the meal in an hour.

"Fifty years, it is true, is but an hour compared with the time you have worked, but with your aid we expect in that time to be able to satisfy some of the hunger that now prevails."

"I do not think that hunger prevails, or that it ever has to any great extent," said Selferedo. "Now and then someone may fail in getting enough to eat, but compared with the whole people the cases are very rare, and if they were known, a supply would be forthcoming. Generally, when such cases do occur, it is the party's own fault, and there is the county house to go to, if nowhere else."

Lovella sighed when she found that Selferedo only thought of physical hunger. "The county house is but a sorry refuge at its best," she said, "but there are other kinds of hunger than that demanding physical food. Heart hunger, soul hunger, spiritual starvation prevail everywhere, and these result from a lack of balance in social relations, and from our ignorance of the finer forces of nature in their adaptation to soul needs."

Selferedo seemed very much surprised at the idea of spiritual starvation. "Why, really," he said, "I cannot understand you. Spiritual starvation, and church spires pointing heavenward from every village in the country? Surely, we are a very religious people."

As he said this, something wonderful occurred— something that made me think of the magicians of Egypt. Lovella waved her hand and there appeared before us a most loathsome and disgusting scene, brutal men, degraded women, ragged children contending for the garbage that had been gathered from the streets. It was a scene from one of the slums of the metropolis of our country, as I afterwards learned.

"Look," she said. He did look and shuddered at the sight.

"How much spirituality is there in the churches when such places as that can exist almost beneath their very shadow?" she asked.

"And do you expect to purify such places as that?" he asked in reply.

"We expect to try and that you will help us. In your haste to evolve great things you have knocked down and trampled upon my weaker children. The churches have no healing for such as these; not that their intent is not good enough, but they don't know how; they do not understand causes. These are among the things to be investigated; these poor wrecks are the ones that the spirit of motherhood must heal as far as is possible, and, at the same time, must find out and remove the causes that have produced such results."

The conversation had so far been carried on between Lovella and Selferedo, but Lovella now turned to the others and said: "We will now look upon some of the grand things that man has done." As she spoke, there unrolled before their gaze immense forests that slowly changed into fertile fields, wigwams that gave place to comfortable dwellings, and still the change went on, till large cities, magnificent residences, storehouses filled with the choicest products of all lands, wonderful architecture, elevated railroads, hanging bridges, magnificent steamers, marvelous machinery, railroads upon which palace cars were gliding, telegraph and telephone lines, these were among the many things shown.

The glorious works of the artist, panoramas of scenes that were past or in some other part of the globe, all these and more, to please the eye and charm the heart, while the rich melody of music and song ravished the ear and enthused the soul—all these, and more than words can express, were shown with wonderful distinctness, while in and out were moving with stately tread, or flitting, dancing along, noble looking men, beautiful women and lovely children, all robed in rich garments, and all fair to look upon.

And in contrast with each of these achievements of man's skill, there came along beside them pictures of what had originally been of the savage condition from which all this had been evolved. It was grand, and Selferedo's eye kindled as he looked, and then turning to the others, he said:

"With all these achievements of man so illustrated before us, in view of all this, we are now asked, have pledged ourselves, to give to woman the lead. What has woman done to deserve such a concession?"

At this the men present began to murmur.

"Wait," said Lovella, "there is another side to this question. The men who have done all this—all and much more than has been shown us, have all been borne beneath woman's heart, have been fed from her bosom and dandled upon her knees, while these, her sons, have assumed to rule over her, refusing to give her a voice in their counsels; is this just, my brothers?"

"It is not just," responded the women, but the men were silent. They ceased to murmur, however, because woman was given a trial leadership, while first one woman then another made some such remarks as these:

"I wonder how much of all this the men would have done if they had had the children to take care of?" "Haven't we always stood by them, cared for them when sick and encouraged them when well? We surely deserve a share of the credit." "Credit or no credit, they couldn't do without us, could you?" said the last speaker, turning toward them a smiling face.

"We shouldn't like to try it," was the general response, and then one of them remarked: "We are waiting to have our work mapped out for us."

"That in good time," said Lovella. "There is enough to be done, but we must go to work advisedly. The work of the past that has succeeded was man's to do, and he has done it in his own way, not under woman's direction; on the other hand, the work that woman can do, has tried to do and has succeeded so poorly in the trying, has had to be done in man's way, and while contending with the adverse conditions which he has furnished. Civilization as it exists today reflects man, not woman. I have shown you some of the grand things that man has done; I will now show you some other things—things that have resulted from the lack of the mother element in his work." Then there came into our range of vision, one by one, scenes that I can never forget. Dear Reader, I am glad you did not see them, for to see and not be able to relieve is torture.

But having seen I must try to tell you, though words can but feebly express the misery thus portrayed. If the enlightened direction of mother love cannot change all this, then there is no hope.

Lovella looked very sad when she proposed to show the other side of the picture, but after a little hesitation, as if debating where to begin, there filed before me, before those assembled in that room, thousands of the most wretched looking women I ever saw, and upon whose foreheads was written the word, "prostitute," but above that and traced by some friendly hand, was written, "victim."

"Prostitutes!" I exclaimed, looking at Lovella. "I thought that woman abolished prostitution at the time of what was called the 'Strike of a Sex.' "

"Look again, and carefully," was the reply; then, as I turned to watch the long procession, I saw what I had not noticed before, a tablet upon the breast of each giving the causes that had brought them into this condition.

I found that about one out of ten of the whole number, being born with strongly passionate natures, and not finding satisfaction by marrying, had chosen this life in preference to the tortures of celibacy, or the unsatisfactory relief of solitary vice. These looked healthier and happier than the others, but far from being satisfied with their lot.

Of the others, about four-tenths had been driven to desperation by man's perfidy, and, cast out by society, had rushed into prostitution as the only thing left them. The remaining half had been driven to it by want, and sold themselves to keep from starvation, to feed their hungry children, or perhaps an aged parent; in some cases all three were combined.

There were cases in which a loved but helpless companion was thus furnished with some comfort while the means by which it was obtained was carefully hidden from the sufferer, the woman thus becoming a veritable sacrifice to love, and beyond what man is capable of, Christ-souls in woman bodies, martyred with the supremest martyrdom possible to human beings; nailed alive to that of which the cross is but a symbol, the masculine organ of generation.

As Lovella noted my thought she said: "Man may be nailed to a wooden cross with spikes of iron, but woman groans from the torture inflicted by a cross of flesh and blood."

Her earnestness awed me, and my heart went out in a great wave of pity toward this unfortunate class of my sisters; for in all that I saw, in the lowest degradations I witnessed, I realized the truth of what the apostle Paul said. I accepted the spirit thereof though I should word it differently. He said: "but for the grace of God." I say: but for different conditions, surroundings and motive powers brought to bear, I might have sunk to the level of the lowest."

When I had fully noted the causes that crowd women into prostitution, Lovella asked, "Can you see now why woman cannot abolish this curse?"

I looked at her in a sort of dazed way, for though partially sensing the reason I could not put it into words.

"It is the economic problem," she said. "Man controls the bread and butter question; that must be rightly adjusted first."

"But," said I, "woman's right to herself puts it in her power to demand such adjustment; she can refuse herself to man till he makes it."

"True, but they have conceded to us half a century of leadership, together with their sympathy and aid, and that is much better than an attempt to force matters in the way you suggest. Many children, more than the entire population of today, will be born in that time, and some of the firstborn will have children, and even grandchildren.

All these children will be gestated under the influence of, and with the idea of 'women in the lead,' and will grow under the influence of the mutual searching for the causes which produce the evils which so mar our grand civilization—searching with the full determination of removing them. Such children will be a radical improvement upon those gestated and born under the influence of the old ideas, and surely that is a much better way of doing than to stand aloof and demand what man himself does not yet know how to grant."

Selferedo listened intently to what Lovella was saying and I saw from the change in his countenance that this power of heredity had not entered into his calculations, and his thought was: "Here is a new factor, one that we must neutralize in some way or she will beat us yet," and he centered his hopes on hurrying up, overdoing the matter. "Come," said he, "this philosophizing is all very fine, but when are we to get to work?"

"We have already begun our work," she smilingly replied. "Men of sense build their homes ideally first— build them in their brains before putting them into visible shape, and women must act with equal discretion. We have a great work to do, and it must be idealized in detail before it can be actualized. Don't hurry us; we have awaited your motion for ages, now please give us our own time."

"That would do if you had ages at your command, but unless you demonstrate your fitness for leadership, you must resign at the end of fifty years."

"And would you be sorry to resume your old position?" she asked.

He turned away with the first impatient movement I had noticed since he was forced to yield to the demand that war should cease. I think Lovella understood him though she gave no sign that would indicate it.

CHAPTER V

The next group that passed before us was that of unhappy wives—wives who submitted to husbands rather than incur greater evils. Women who were so situated that they must part with their children and go out homeless or yield in opposition to their own feelings. The greater portion of these were from the laboring classes, and as I looked upon their hollow eyes and sunken cheeks, as I saw that their faded appearance was the result of overwork and bearing unwelcome children, and as the effect of such conditions upon their children were clearly shown me, I cried out in an agony of protest.

"Is this the outcome of the pledge that woman should own herself?"

"Do you not know," said Lovella, "that one may keep the letter of a pledge and yet violate its spirit? Our best, our noblest men, such as we may safely counsel with in reference to the great work to be done, will keep the spirit of that pledge. They will hold not only the persons of their wives, but their own persons sacred. They will continue their respectful, lover-like attentions and await the pleasure of their companions, realizing that mutuality is far more satisfactory than enforced claims; they will thus preserve, instead of destroy, the attraction which first drew them together."

"But what about the others?" I asked. "How is it that they can obey the letter and yet so violate the spirit of their pledge?"

"I do not suppose," she replied, "that the husbands of those unhappy wives, those unwilling mothers, have insisted upon obedience to their desires. They have made no demands so far as the letter of a demand is concerned, but with a sort of lordly indifference they have said, by their manner if not in words, do as you please, I make no claims. But if you are free, I am; I can find other women who will accept me, women who need my aid and I cannot support more than one. She knows that he can make her utterly wretched even if he does not drive her from his home and put another in her place, thus separating her from her children, so she yields to what seems to her the lesser evil because she has not the courage to face the consequences of a refusal. He has made no claims upon her, of course he hasn't, but he has compelled her to submit all the same.

She paused and looked at me in a way which made me feel that she desired some expression from me as to where the trouble lay.

"It seems to me," I said in reply, "that this evil, like the other, is rooted in our false system of property relations. Those whose toil produces the wealth of the world do not get their share."

"Then what is to be done?"

"The system itself must be changed; there is no other way."

Lovella then turned to the others: "You have heard the reply; is it correct?"

The women and a majority of the men replied in the affirmative, while the others remained silent and thoughtful.

At this point Selferedo said: "There certainly can be some method of adjusting things without making such an entire change as your remarks seem to indicate."

"Please find such a method and show its feasibility and we shall only be too glad to adopt it," replied Lovella.

"Would not a plentiful supply of legal tender currency make business brisk, wages good and furnish employment for many hands that are now idle? This would apply to woman as well as man, as women now do almost everything that men do, and that certainly would give them a chance to avoid prostitution if they so chose, and it would greatly relieve the other conditions of which you speak."

Lovella was silent for so long a time that Selferedo seemed to imagine that she could find no objections to what he had suggested, but just as he was about to reinforce his views with additional arguments she said:

"Those who now possess the wealth would find a way to divert the surplus increase to themselves, and the wage laborer would still be tributary—would still be a wage slave, and slaves, as such, can never become cultured, refined, or morally elevated."

"But why, madam, would the increase necessarily go to the already rich?"

"Upon the same principle that additional blood in an already congested human body would surely rush to the congested part. Our economic body is congested; the first thing to do is to restore the equilibrium. If the two kindred evils which have been portrayed before us were the only ones rooted in economic congestion, there might be some faint hope of an adjustment, but there are others to be considered. We will now look upon another scene in which it is woman that is still the sufferer."

As she said this, I looked a little to the left of where I was standing, and I saw an immense multitude of women of all ages. As they marched slowly by, I noted that each one plied a needle, a sewing machine, or both, and what was more strange, each one carried with her an exact reflection of her surroundings. Near some were fireless rooms and hungry, crying children. Now and then these would snatch a crust of bread or some broken meat or cold, perhaps raw potatoes and divide it among the crying ones, reserving the smallest portion for themselves, and then work with renewed speed as if to make up for lost time.

Then again these would wrap the children in the poor apology for bed clothes and hurry out to get the poor pittance for their toil with which to buy a little coal and a little food, being careful always, if possible, to save something towards the rent. On, on they went, till the line stretched far beyond my range of vision, and still they came, a hungry, gaunt, sorrowful multitude, many of them working upon rich garments, while the plainest, coarsest of those upon which others stitched were better than they themselves could wear.

As one hollow-eyed woman passed, I felt a strange sensation, and looking to learn what it meant, I saw lines that connected her with the cloak I wore. "She made it. A portion of her life has gone into it," was my thought, and then such a wave of sadness, of gloom came flowing in upon those lines of connection and enveloped me as it were. It was just what she had felt while making the cloak.

Quick as thought the question came to me: "Suppose you were a wife and soon to be a mother, would not this feeling be woven into the very life of your child?"

"Oh heaven, is this possible!" Lovella saw and understood:

"Yes," she replied, "it is more than possible. The rich cannot escape the results of the conditions imposed upon the poor. People recognize the fact that the germs of physical disease may be carried in clothing or bedding, but fail to recognize the equally important truth that moral disease can be communicated in the same way, and that in some cases it may thus become a hereditary endowment for evil."

I can never forget the feeling of yearning horror that came over me—an inexpressible pity and a yearning to take them out of such horrible conditions. Lovella, as usual, read my thought and said in response:

"And we must do it, it is a part of our work. It is because of this, that these scenes are thus portrayed. To do so simply to shock the beholder's feelings would be cruelty, but in the end we expect, intend to do away with all such conditions."

"In fifty years?" asked Selferedo in an incredulous tone.

"Why not?" she replied, turning her luminous eyes full upon him. "The materials are prepared for the new structure, they need only to be rightly adjusted."

"Ah, the materials, you give us that much credit?"

"Most certainly, and we credit your further ability by acknowledging our need of your committed effort."

"As your servants," he replied, bowing to hide the mocking smile that wreathed his lips.

"Why not?" she again asked. "Did not he who is claimed as 'the Master,' say 'He that is greatest among you, let him be your servant'?" There was a smile upon the faces of those present at this reply, and Selferedo said no more, but one of the men who was in sympathy with him remarked:

"I suppose you will say that these also are the victims of our economic system."

"Well, are they not?" she asked.

"I cannot see, madam, how the system can be charged with the results of the selfishness of employers."

"The system is at fault, my dear sir, because it leaves the fate of the employee in the employer's hands. Any system which allows one class of people to make it impossible for another class to have direct access to the sources of supply is a false one, not only because of the dependence it involves, but because the natural tendency of such a system is to make the dominant class selfish and tyrannical."

"You make a good people's advocate," was the only reply, and he also took refuge in silence, and still the hollow-eyed, sad-faced women continued to file past.

"Will they never have done?" said another impatiently.

102

At this there dropped over them something that was like a veil, thus hiding them from our sight, but Lovella said:

"As long as time lasts they must continue their march unless something is done to remove the causes which make them what they are, but there are other armies of sufferers that we must look upon in order to get some idea of the magnitude of our work," and then there came thousands upon thousands of men, and some women, who were reeling and staggering with drunkenness.

Oh, the sickening sight! Blear-eyed, bloated, pale; haggard, blasphemous and obscene songs, curses and cunning leers, desperation, imbecility, shrieks, stolidity, each phase terrible in itself, but when thus combined the scene beggared description.

"That surely," said Selferedo, "is not the result of our economic system. Those men are not obliged to drink unless they choose."

"And what would be your remedy?" asked Lovella.

"I would imprison every man who drank to excess."

"Do you believe there is any truth in the sciences of physiology and phrenology?" she continued.

"Certainly, but as yet they are far from being perfect."

"True, but I would like to have those for whom you propose a prison examined by as competent physiologists and phrenologists as we have. I feel very certain that some physical or moral defect, perhaps both, would be found in every one of them."

"And you would therefore consider them irresponsible, is that what you mean?"

"In a measure, yes."

"That will not do, Lovella, some of the most noted men that have lived, died drunkards."

"And noted, talented men and women have died insane, sire, but there was some unbalanced brain condition or body reacting upon the brain, which, when a pressure was brought to bear, could not stand the strain, and this is equally true of the drunkard. When we have a knowledge of what perfect motherhood should be, and the conditions to carry it out, we shall have no drunkards and no insane people."

"You claim a great deal for motherhood, madam."

"There is a text of scripture, sir, which says: 'The seed of a woman shall bruise the serpent's head.' Did you ever read it?"

"Most assuredly I have, but I cannot see what possible application that can have to the subject at hand."

"But what meaning do you attach to the text, Selferedo?"

"I—I have not thought much about it; the Christian world claims Jesus as the seed of the woman."

"The Christian world has attached certain meanings to many things which a more extended knowledge has shown to be capable of much broader interpretations, and in this case I do not think it will be very difficult to show the application to the subject at hand."

"And he is not so much to blame for this; he is held to that plane of life by conditions he cannot break. His daily life is not his own. It is not the love of accomplishing—of evolving works of use or pleasure—that sends him about his daily toil, not the love of the work of which others have the results, all but a mere subsistence, but hard necessity which holds him to it.

"He has no time to spend in intellectual enjoyment or to cultivate an esthetic taste. Only purely sensuous enjoyment—and that in its crudest form—is at his command, and his poor wife must be made to minister to that while the coarseness of its expression repels her and destroys her power to reciprocate his passion, if indeed a chronic state of sexual hunger can properly be called passion. Poor man, he is to be pitied. Poor wife and poorly organized children—double victims, victims of victims, and what is to be done?

"Such men know nothing of the tender care which, cultivating the rich fruits of the garden of love, renders them an increasing and perpetual delight, and thus they generally crush the life out of earth's purest joys, leaving only fierce fires and ashes. What can be done to change all this, think you?"

"It seems to me," I said, "that it will take time, education, culture."

"Yes, it will take time, but how much time have these poor people to devote to culture, and what chance is there under such conditions that children will be born capable of a high state of cultivation when born of mothers who must toil during the day to the last point of endurance, and then satisfy, or try to, the husband's merely animal desire at night—merely animal desire because the conditions do not admit of any higher feeling—and this during all the time that the poor wife is, from her own poorly cared for body, feeding another life? Besides, what kind of influences do her surroundings send along the line of her nerves to the coming one? Garrets, cellars, bare walls, coarse food and clothing are not very likely to furnish the elements for a high order of offspring."

"Well, please give us your interpretation," he said with an indulgent smile, such as self-conceited men often bestow upon woman while listening to her ideas.

Lovella took no notice of this, but proceeded to comply with the request. "Civilization," she said, "is the result more of man's efforts than of woman's; not only is society as it exists today his child, but the law also gives to him the children that woman bears. They are legally his, and they are his too by the quality of their natures, because they are gestated and born under conditions that he furnishes. They are not the seed of the woman; the serpent's head, figuratively speaking, is everywhere apparent.

"Now when our sex revolution is fully accomplished, then motherhood will come to the front. The children will then be hers. Then she will see to it that a knowledge of our own bodies and brains, together with that of the conditions under which perfect motherhood can be actualized, will see to it that such knowledge shall take precedence over all else. Then the seed of the woman shall bruise the serpent's head, and not till then.

"Now," she continued, "if you can show that our property system has not interfered with the best conditions for motherhood, then I will admit that it has had nothing to do with the condition of these," waving her hand towards the still passing wrecks of manhood and womanhood.

"The liquor traffic interferes far more with the conditions for perfect motherhood than does our economic system," was his reply to this.

"That the liquor traffic intensifies the evil cannot be denied," said Lovella, thoughtfully, "but our laboring men do not all drink, nor do all the men who are reduced to the lowest degree of poverty. Yet the results to motherhood in such cases are nonetheless disastrous. But suppose it can be shown that the traffic itself, the greater part of it, is the result of the system which makes the pursuit of wealth of paramount importance, what then?"

Selferedo made no direct reply to this; as to my own feelings, the most bitter thought of all was that what I had witnessed represented facts, that though the wretched ones I had seen were not exactly in marching lines, they were even much more numerous than there represented.

CHAPTER VI

Hitherto, with the exception of Lovella and myself, only the men had spoken, and aside from Selferedo, but two of them, but at this point one of the women remarked:

"It seems to me that prohibitory laws enforcing a stop to the manufacture of intoxicating drinks would settle that question, and in view of the importance of the right conditions for motherhood, the fact that intoxicants are so destructive of all that makes a mother's work a blessing should be sufficient reason for the enactment of such a law."

Like a flash the army of drunkards disappeared, and in its place stood a large city through the streets of which marched an army of women carrying flags and banners. On the latter were various inscriptions which read: "Down with the saloons." "Five thousand dens of destruction, away with them." "Two and a half million dollars paid annually for license to sell liquid fire." "Think of the cost to the people of five thousand saloons, and who pays it?" "What's to be done?" "The saloon must go." On they went with determination written upon their faces, and I watched till I saw every saloon closed.

"Oh, I am so glad!" I exclaimed involuntarily.

"Wait," said Lovella, and then the scene changed. As all liquors were worthless now, could not be sold at any price, it followed as a matter of course that the five thousand saloon keepers, together with the wholesale liquor dealers, were now deprived of their means of support. We were next shown these with their wives and children, not less than twenty-five thousand people, all anxiously asking how they were going to live.

The most of them had been rendered utterly poor. True, some few owned the houses in which they lived, but now the taxes would be much heavier; for the two and a half millions of license money which had helped to defray the expenses of the city government must be raised by increased taxation, and how long would their homes be theirs with no means of self-support?

This was a side of the question I had not thought of. Lovella seemed to possess the power of illuminating that which she wished to teach. She said not a word as by a wave of her hand one scene after another was brought before us. More than five thousand men wanting employment and not five hundred vacant places in the whole city, and these but temporarily, for there were enough others to more than fill them, others much better qualified than an ex-saloon keeper would be, and what was to be done?

The first scene placed before us in answer to this inquiry was the home of a man who supported a wife and six children from the proceeds of a corner grocery. His rent was very high, but it would now be higher. The taxes being increased, those who had houses to rent would add the tax to the price demanded for their use. It was all he could do now to live; and if the ex-saloon keeper on the opposite corner took up the grocery business, he must go under. There was no help for it.

He did not speak, but by some occult law his thoughts were made visible. The ex-saloon man did start a grocery upon a small scale. He must do something in order to live, and he trusted to his customers in the old business to patronize him in this. He struggled along nearly a year and then failed, but not till the competition, the division of the trade had so involved the old grocery keeper that he could not rally.

On, on we followed this family from one downward step in misfortune to another. Having lost his hold, the man could not regain his footing; finally, with his wife dead and his children scattered, he filled a suicide's grave. True his fate was no worse than that of many, the cause of which could be traced to saloons, and the woman who had advised the prohibitory law said as much. Lovella replied, and most emphatically:

"WE WANT A CURE, NOT A CHANGE OF EVILS."

The next scene shown us was the career of the ex-saloon keeper. Slowly it was unrolled at one end and rolled up at the other till at last the man sat with a kit of burglar's tools by his side, and in reply to his wife's remonstrance he said: "I cannot see you and the children starve, and everything else that I have tried has failed. By some sort of hocus pocus some people get all there is, and if I am sharp enough to get some of it back I don't see that I am so much worse than other folks."

Next we saw the family gathering up their household goods and taking a western train. We saw the husband

and the oldest son leave at the first station and return to the city in disguise; we saw them go to the house of a rich merchant who was known to be absent, and entering by means of their burglar's tools, gather together such valuables as they could find. They hoped to get away without being discovered, but when they left, two women lay dead upon the floor and the house was on fire. They escaped and were never traced.

"Now," said Lovella, when this last scene disappeared, "multiply these cases, with varying shades of detail, a thousand fold and you will have some of the results of a forced closing of the saloons *under* our present property system. You may think the pictures overdrawn, but I can assure you they are not."

"Then you would leave the liquor traffic untouched," said Selferedo.

"I would go to the root of things and remove the causes which create a demand for liquor and then the traffic would cease of itself; but there is yet more to be shown of the results of an enforced morality," and again she waved her hand.

There now came into view some fifty cottages occupied and partly owned by laboring men. These homes were being paid for in monthly installments, and with no bad luck would in another year be wholly theirs. Not one of these men drank, and but few of them used tobacco. I felt a shrinking as I gazed, for with the previous scenes before my mind I sensed what was coming.

Presently I saw those men returning from their work with saddened faces. They tried to put on a smile as they entered their homes, but their wives saw that something was the matter and began to question them. Then it all came out:

The ex-saloon men, in order to get work, were underbidding them, unless they would consent to work for less wages, they were likely to lose their places and with them all hope of paying for their homes. If they consented to work for less they could still secure bread for themselves and their families, but the prospect of saving their homes was but little better.

It seemed to me that I could bear no more. The idea of those men losing their homes went through me like a knife. But the worst part of it was I could see that such a result was but the natural sequence of our economic law under such circumstances. If our earnest workers for reform would only try to trace the reaction as well as the action of the forces they set in motion, they would work to better purpose, because they would work more wisely than they now do.

We were shown a few more scenes all involving the same lesson and then Lovella said:

"In the scene wherein the laboring men were shown to be in danger of losing their homes, together with others thus affected, you may multiply your fifty by thirty and not overstate the number of homes lost to honest worthy men because of the breaking up of conditions caused by forcibly closing the saloons in one city only. When the whole cost is counted, when all who suffer by this change are considered, you will find that the evil designed to be removed presents itself in other forms and the sum of the misery produced is even greater than before.

"True, there are many, very many cases of rejoicing, scenes of gladness which, if portrayed, and the other side not shown, would be considered unanswerable evidence of the great good done by closing the saloons, but what we want is to *heal* this our great human patient. This—driving the disease from one part of the body to another

"IS NOT A CURE"

"But you do not tell us what should be done," said one of the two men who had before spoken.

"Too many have told that before they found out themselves, and I am willing to wait a little; besides if I knew exactly the true and only method, I would only give out at first such hints as would set others to searching for the better way, as I should want a great deal of *intelligent* assistance.

"You must remember," she continued, "that work well done is twice done. This subject must be thoroughly understood before we can adopt measures that will secure success. I might show you in succession the vast armies of the insane, the idiotic, the blind, the deaf and dumb, and bring up the rear with the long, long train of those who fill our poorhouses and our prisons, but you have already seen enough of society's wrecks. Rest assured, however, that any method which does not reach all those will be work half done, consequently not done at all."

"Men point with pride to the asylums they furnish for human wrecks, thinking it an evidence of great humanity on their part. They do not realize in the least the shame of there being a need for such asylums. When the conditions for perfect motherhood are secured, there will be no such need, but until woman revolutionizes society, such conditions cannot be had.

"Now," she said in conclusion, "it is my wish that those present, acting upon the lines of thought here indicated, shall go forth and study the workings of society in all its parts, that you may arm yourselves with the truths which will enable us to accomplish the revolution contemplated. Go singly, two by two, or in groups, but be watchful, careful, wise, and determined that no present nor personal interest shall for a moment blind your judgment.

"Do this, remembering what it is that you are undertaking. If you cannot solve the problem, if there cannot be formulated and put into practice a system of society which will not grind up one portion of its members for the benefit of other portions, then we might as well cease trying to do for others. The only thing left us will be to make the most of ourselves individually, and let those who cannot stand the pressure go down to be ground over in the evolution of the eternities.

"Study this question for the next five years, and then meet here to report. Till then, adieu."

The scene vanished and I found myself where I had lain down to rest after reading "The Strike of a Sex."

I lay for some minutes in a half-dazed condition with Lovella's last words still ringing in my ear. "Yes," I said aloud, "I will go with the others," and that fully awakened me.

More Resources From
New Society Publishers

To Order: send check or money order to New Society
Publishers, 4722 Baltimore Avenue, Philadelphia, PA
19143. For postage and handling: add $1.50 for the first
book and 40 cents for each additional book.

NO TURNING BACK: LESBIAN AND GAY LIBERATION FOR THE '80s

by Gerre Goodman, George Lakey, Judy Lashof and Erika Thorne

Foreword by Malcolm Boyd

"This is the place where the lesbian/gay movement must be."

> Harry Britt,
> Board of Supervisors,
> City and County of San Francisco

"*No Turning Back* fulfills a long felt need for a progressive analysis and pragmatic sourcebook for lesbians, gays and others concerned with replacing patriarchal oppression with a more human alternative. I was quite pleased by the integration of personal statements and experiences into the more theoretical discussion, and by the inclusion of practical and feasible proposals for individual and collective action."

> Larry Gross,
> Professor, Annenberg School of Communications
> University of Pennsylvania; and Co-Chairperson
> Philadelphia Lesbian and Gay Task Force

This book is recommended for academic and larger public libraries by LIBRARY JOURNAL.

168 Pages.
Hardcover: $16.95
Paperback: $7.95

"A hardy, necessary, lived voice."

—Susan Griffin

OUR STUNNING HARVEST
Poems by Ellen Bass
Foreword by Florence Howe

"The poems are rich with natural images, sensual and pungent; rich too because they are powerfully rooted in a woman's body and love."

—Marge Piercy

"These poems are sustaining and important for they enhance our sense of life and its meaning, our hold on life. We must see that they reach many. For earthly, for beautiful, survival."

—Tillie Olsen

Ellen Bass won the Elliston Book Award for Poetry, and is co-editor of *No More Masks! An Anthology of Poems by Women* (Doubleday) and *I Never Told Anyone: Writings by Women Survivors of Child Sexual Abuse* (Harper & Row). Her poem "Our Stunning Harvest", which appeared in *Reweaving the Web of Life: Feminism and Nonviolence,* has been read and performed nation-wide by women and anti-nuclear activists.

112 pages. 1985.
Hardcover: $19.95
Paperback: $6.95

A special deluxe edition of *Our Stunning Harvest* is available from Moving Parts Press, 419A Maple Street, Santa Cruz, CA 95060.

WOMEN IN DEVELOPMENT: A RESOURCE GUIDE FOR ORGANIZATION AND ACTION

by ISIS Women's International Information and Communication Service.

A lavishly illustrated book, with 122 photographs, five years in the making. Women scholars from all over the world contributed to make this one of the most comprehensive and beautiful books of its kind ever published. Sections on women and multinationals, women and rural development, women and health, education, tourism, migration, etc.

Annotated resource lists, bibliographies. 240 pages. 1984.

Hardcover: $39.95

Paperback: $14.95

WE ARE ALL PART OF ONE ANOTHER: A BARBARA DEMING READER

edited with an introduction by Jane Meyerding
Foreword by Barbara Smith

Essays, speeches, letters, stories, poems by America's foremost writer on issues of women and peace, feminism and nonviolence, spanning four decades.

"Barbara Deming always challenges us to rise above easy answers about who we are. Her insight into the nature of political change and the needs of the human spirit makes hers a unique feminist voice which guides and inspires us in the struggle for a more humane world."

—Charlotte Bunch

"Her work continues to be life-sustaining, as necessary as breath to me. This new collection is indeed a treasure."

—Pam McAllister

320 pages. 1984.
Hardcover: $24.95
Paperback: $10.95

REWEAVING THE WEB OF LIFE: FEMINISM AND NONVIOLENCE
edited by Pam McAllister

". . . happens to be one of the most important books you'll ever read."

—*The Village Voice*

"Stressing the connection between patriarchy and war, sex and violence, this book shows that nonviolence can be an assertive, positive force. It's provocative reading for anyone interested in surviving and changing the nuclear age."

—*Ms. Magazine*

More than 50 contributors. Topics include: Women's History, Women and the Struggle Against Militarism, Violence and its Origins, Nonviolence and Women's Self-Defense. A richly varied collection of interviews, songs, poems, stories, provocative proposals, photographs.

Most often recommended book in the 1983 WIN MAGAZINE ANNUAL BOOK POLL

Annotated Bibliography. Index.
448 pages.
Hardcover: $19.95
Paperback: $10.95

THE EYE OF THE CHILD
by Ruth Mueller

A brilliant healing myth for a world gone mad!

"Of all the creatures to whom the great mother had given birth all were a part, not apart, but one. Yes all but one flowed as she flowed, born of her womb, dying in her bosom, struggling, true, but never against their own life support. One, only one, capable of standing apart, imagining self above and outside, turning to rend, turning to overpower, to subdue, to conquer the vessel of life itself, creation's own embodiment. Had she not labored for aeons to give birth to a triumph of joy and beauty as fair as dawn, a creature of light to share the glowing consciousness of the whole, one of understanding as deep as her deeps are deep, of laughter as divine as tears and of tears as cleansing as laughter, one who was no alien to mercy, capable of new visions above predation, a familiar to the art of healing, above all a creature of tongues, creation itself no longer mute to express—to express—

What had gone wrong?"

Ecological speculative fiction of the highest order.

240 pages. 1985.
Paperback: $7.96

"This is the bravest book I have read since Jonathan Schell's FATE OF THE EARTH."

—Dr. Rollo May

DESPAIR AND PERSONAL POWER IN THE NUCLEAR AGE
by Joanna Rogers Macy

Despair and Personal Power in the Nuclear Age is the first major book to examine our psychological responses to planetary perils and to lay the theoretical foundations for an empowering, personally-centered approach to social change. Included are sections on awakening in the nuclear age, relating to children and young people, guided meditations, empowered rituals, and a special section on "Spiritual Exercises for a Time of Apocalypse." This book was described and excerpted in *New Age Journal* and *Fellowship Magazine*, recommended for public libraries by *Library Journal*, and selected for inclusion in the 1984 Women's Reading Program, General Board of Global Ministries, United Methodist Church.

200 pages. Appendices, resource lists, exercises. 1983.
Hardcover: $19.95
Paperback: $8.95